Lois Smith Brady is the author of:

Vows: Weddings of the Nineties

from <u>The New York Times</u>

Lois
Smith Brady

Simon & Schuster

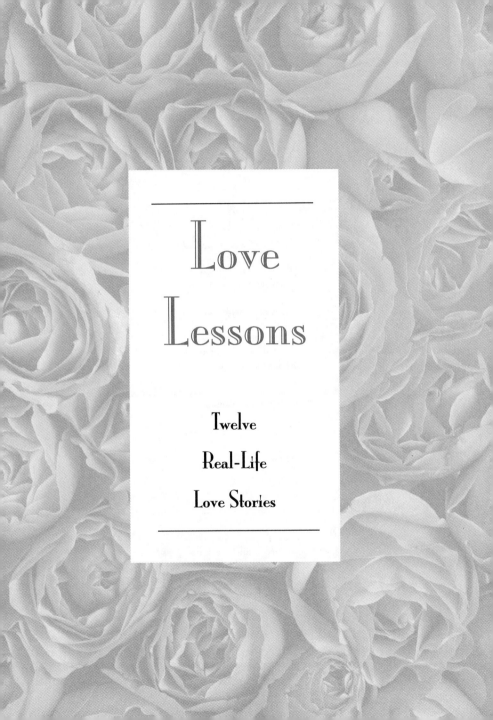

Love
Lessons

Twelve
Real-Life
Love Stories

SIMON & SCHUSTER
Rockefeller Center
1230 Avenue of the Americas
New York, NY 10020

Copyright © 1999 by Lois Smith Brady

Designed by Katy Riegel

Manufactured in the United States of America

3   5   7   9   10   8   6   4   2

Library of Congress Cataloging-in-Publication Data

Brady, Lois Smith.
Love lessons : twelve real-life love stories / Lois Smith Brady.
p.   cm.
1. Love—Case studies.   2. Man-woman relationships—Case studies.   I. Title.
BF575.L8B69   1999
306.7'092'2—dc21   99-13485
                                                              CIP

ISBN 0-684-85234-9

THIS BOOK IS dedicated to my husband, Tom Van Allen. I knew he was the one when we first traveled on an airplane together. I'm terrified of flying, and he was able to distract me completely by talking about the various virtues of his former girlfriends.

And to our sons, Will and Charlie. I love them down to their eyelashes.

And to my parents, William and Lois Brady, who taught me my first love lessons.

Contents

Introduction
15

The Boy Next Door
Madeline and Morty
35

Soul Mates On-line
Susie and Randy
53

Cloudland
Lois and Bill
69

Contents

Muddy Waters
Ellen and Eddy
83

Love Is Blind
Richelle and William
99

A Potluck Romance
Alison and Pete
115

Diehard Bachelor Meets Single Mom
Susan and Rick
133

The Ultimate Adventure
Mel and Chris
151

A Magnificent Hunch
Holly and David
167

Timing Is Everything
Linda and Andre
183

Contents

Love at First Sight
Paisley and Karl
199

Green Bananas
Clarice and Victor
217

Photo Credits
233

Acknowledgments
235

LOVE COMES in all packages and sizes. I've seen love that was slow to happen and love that was instant. I've seen couples who were friends a long time and suddenly it turned to romance. I've seen couples with similar interests and ones who were extremely different, but still, there was that spark, that profound connection. Although their experiences may be totally different, they see the world in the same way. They say, "I know . . . I know!"

—Lois Kellerman,
Ethical Culture Leader

Introduction

I FIRST BEGAN to learn about love in dancing school, at the age of twelve. My waltzing and fox-trot lessons took place in a daffodil-yellow ballroom in my hometown of Chestnut Hill, Pennsylvania, a place full of cobblestone roads, Gothic houses, emerald-green soccer fields, and wood-paneled station wagons. When I arrived at dancing class on the first day, I remember feeling like a princess floating on a cloud. I thought I was going to fall madly in love with one of the boys in class and spend the next years of my life kissing and waltzing. Before long, though, I felt more like someone standing under a dark thundercloud.

During class, I sat among the girls, on one side of the room, waiting for a boy to ask me to dance. To my complete shock, I was consistently one of the last to be asked.

At first, I thought the boys had made a terrible mistake. I was so funny and pretty, I remember thinking, I could beat everyone I knew at tennis, could climb trees faster than a cat, and blow perfect smoke rings. Why didn't they dash toward me?

My overconfidence lasted about as long as a smoke ring in the rain, and I have never really regained it. Class after class, I watched the boys in blue blazers and gray pants head toward girls in flowered shifts whose perfect ponytails swung back and forth like metronomes. They fell easily into step with each other in a way that seemed completely mysterious to me. I was someone who always had scraped knees, and watching them week after week, I came to believe that love belonged only to those who glided, those who never tripped, fell, shimmied up trees, or even really touched the ground. By the time I was thirteen, I knew how to subtly tilt my head and make my tears fall back into my eyes, instead of down my cheeks, when no one asked me to dance.

Around that time, I discovered the "powder room," which became my pink, softly lit, reliable retreat. Whenever I started to cry, I'd excuse myself and run in there. Ever since, I have used the powder room, or ladies' room, for recovering in almost every kind of situation—avoiding old boyfriends at parties, constructing sentences that might make me sound wittier at dinners, looking in the mirror and taking account of my life as people laughed loudly at a cocktail party right outside the door, or sitting out bad turbulence on airplanes.

In dancing school, it took years for me to stop crying. It wasn't until I met Matt, a blond boy who was at least as unpopular as I was. He was quiet and he always hung out on the edges of the room. When we danced for the first time, he wouldn't even look me in the eyes. But he was very cute, and soon I learned that he told great stories. We became good buddies and loyal partners, dancing every single dance together for years, until dancing school ended. I learned from him my most important early lesson about romance—that the potential for love exists in corners, in the most unlikely as well as the most obvious places.

For many years, my love life continued to be like one long tragicomic novel. In college, I fell in love with a tall English major who rode a motorcycle, had shoulder-length hair, and a face like Bobby Kennedy's. I was crazy about him but he stood me up on our sixth date—an afternoon of skydiving. I ended up jumping out of the airplane alone, feeling the beginnings of a broken heart. Although the first part of the jump went well, I was blown sideways toward the end and landed in a parking lot, right between a Volkswagen bug and a van. That seemed to be the way I always landed when it came to love. Broken hearts, I found, are a lot like broken bones. At first, there's no pain, only shock and a hint of disability, like a house that stands briefly after an earthquake. But then, just when you think you might be okay, you fall apart entirely.

Halfway through college, I took a break to be a ski bum and to look for love in the mountains. I packed some Scandinavian sweaters and a few pairs of jeans, all messy and unfolded, and moved to Sun Valley, Idaho, where a few years earlier I'd kissed a man named Buzz. He was tall and red-headed, and we used to kiss in our down parkas on cross-country skis in deep powder.

He had moved since I met him, to a ranch way outside town with telephone wires that blew down in the winter-time. I never managed to reach him by phone during my stay, but I saw him once by chance, sitting in a café in town with a plain woman who looked like a minister's wife in the nineteenth century. I happened to be eating at a table nearby and I secretly watched Buzz and his companion, trying to figure out if they were in love. They never held hands or kissed, never did anything obvious, so I decided to walk over and say hello.

Of course, I had to go to the ladies' room to get up my nerve and compose my opening sentences. I will always re-member staring at myself in the mirror at that moment, a nineteen-year-old with dirty blond hair, green eyes, a bro-ken heart, and about $300 to my name. My favorite pair of blue jeans had just been stolen from a Laundromat in town. Standing there, I imagined myself living in Sun Valley in a house full of skis and fireplaces, maybe even on the windswept ranch with Buzz. I remember thinking three children was a nice number.

When I walked out of the bathroom, I headed toward Buzz's table, rushing so I wouldn't lose my courage. But he and the woman had left—their plates were still there, along with half-empty water glasses, napkins thrown down like squashed snowballs, and a droopy, sad-looking carnation. It was one of the eeriest moments of my life, like walking outside and finding your car stolen. I can still remember looking for Buzz up and down the road, which was covered with a layer of snow as thick as a down quilt.

I learned another lesson that day—love is chancy, and it can slip your grip like nothing else. Like a ghost, it can scare you to death, reappear and disappear without explanation, and break all the rules of gravity and sense.

In my mid-twenties, I moved to New York City, where love was as hard to find as a legal parking spot. Everyone in New York is obsessed with love. It is a city full of bagels, limousines, skyscrapers, and people with broken hearts. I had plenty of heartbreaks myself while I lived there. My first Valentine's Day set the tone for the next five years. I went out on a date to a crowded surf bar on the Upper West Side, and halfway through dinner my date excused himself and never returned. He vanished. On the way home, I got caught in the middle of a Frisbee game some kids were playing with jagged coffee tin tops. It made perfect sense to me that I might be decapitated that night. At the time, I lived in a walkup apartment with a beautiful roommate. Flowers piled up at our door like snowdrifts, and the answering machine light always blinked in a panicky way, overloaded with messages from her admirers. Limos were forever purring outside our building, with dates waiting behind tinted windows for her. In my mind, love was something behind a tinted window, part apparition, part shadow, definitely unreachable. Whenever I spotted happy-looking couples on the sidewalk, I'd wonder where they found love and want to follow them home for the answer.

After a few years in the city, while living on the top floor of a brownstone where I shared a hall bathroom with a French couple who took bubble baths all day, I got a job writing a weekly column about weddings for a New York City magazine called 7 *Days*. My job was to find interesting engaged couples, interview them, and write up their love stories. It was a dream assignment for me—I got to ask total strangers the questions I'd always wanted to blurt out. The job didn't seem like strict journalism; it was more like extreme nosiness. I finally got to ask people in love, "How long did your first date last and what *exactly* were you thinking of each other?" Or, "How did you know it was love?" Or, "What do you talk about in the middle of the night?" Or, "What was your first kiss like?" First kisses, I've found, are not a good barometer for anything—I've met lots of couples who said their first kiss was about as pleasant as dieting, but who fell madly in love anyway.

I usually interviewed couples in their homes. One week, I might visit two dancers living in a tiny apartment filled with wind chimes and cats, in a crumbling building that lay at the foot of a bridge like an old, squashed Coke can. Then, the next week I'd meet a couple in their ten-room, sprawling apartment where meek maids served me hors d'oeuvres and exotic fruit drinks on silver trays as I asked my questions. Over the years, everyone, from folksingers to fishmongers, filmmakers, lawyers, wilderness guides, private eyes, jewelry designers, composers, and cowboys, has told me their stories of love.

No matter where couples lived, whether there were Picassos or $5 posters on the walls, I learned that true love has some universal qualities and telltale signs. For one thing, most couples I've interviewed said they felt incredibly lucky, even giddy, after meeting—they had an *I-won-the-lottery!* feeling. I interviewed a stewardess once who met her future husband on an airplane. She told me, when you fall in love, you shouldn't have to make a list of pros and cons. You shouldn't have to take the good with the bad. It should be all good news. Whenever anyone asks me about love now, I always say wait for that feeling, wait, wait, wait. Wait with the patience of a Buddhist fly fisherman.

One woman I interviewed compared the experience of falling in love to finding a gilded ballroom on the other side of your small, dingy studio apartment. It's something you never imagined existed, something magical, a little scary when you think about it, and bigger than you ever dreamed. I've come to believe that if you're in love, you should honestly be able to describe your partner this way: "Think of the perfect person. Then, think harder."

Over the years, I have found at least one sure answer to the question, How do you know it's love? You know when the tiny and everyday things surrounding you—the leaves on the ground, the shade of light in the sky, the flowers on the table, the background music, a bowl of strawberries, a message on your answering machine—suddenly shimmer with a kind of unreality. You know when the tiny details about another person, ones that are insignificant or mundane to most people, seem fascinating and incredible to you. One groom told me he loved everything about his future wife, from her handwriting to the way she scratched on their apartment door like a cat when she came home. During another interview, a bride said she fell in love with her fiancé partly because he knew how to repair car engines and frozen pipes, but the fact that he never, ever killed bugs really won her heart. "One night, a moth was flying around a light bulb, and he caught it and let it out the window," she remembered. "I said, 'That's it. He's the guy.'"

You also know it's love when you can't stop talking to each other. Almost every couple I've ever interviewed has said that on their first or second date, they talked for hours and hours and hours—in some cases, days passed before they stopped talking. For some, falling in love is like walking into a soundproof confession booth, a place where you can tell all. I have heard many people say the first conversation is far more important than the first kiss.

While finding love can be like discovering a ballroom on the other side of your tiny apartment, it is at the same time like finding a pair of great old blue jeans that are exactly your size and seem as if you've worn them forever. I cannot tell you how many women have told me they knew they were in love because they forgot to wear makeup around their new boyfriend. Or because they felt comfortable hanging around the house with him in flannel pajamas. There is some modern truth to Cinderella's tale—it's love when you're incredibly comfortable, when the shoe fits perfectly.

Finally, I think you're in love if you can make each other laugh at the very worst moments, like when the IRS is auditing you or when you're driving a convertible in a rainstorm or when your hair is turning gray. Judy Collins, the folksinger, once told me about a time she visited her long-time boyfriend, Louis Nelson, in the hospital. They had been living together for about sixteen years, ever since their first date, but he now had a ruptured appendix and was near death. Still, they managed to crack each other up.

Louis described one of Judy's hospital visits this way: "She held on to me. She brought me crystals and a cross and smiles. She said, all pensive and serious, 'We should get married.' I said, in a Demerol fog, 'That won't keep me from dying.'"

As someone once told me, ninety percent of being in love is making each other's lives funnier and easier, all the way to the deathbed.

Seven years ago, I started writing about love and weddings for *The New York Times* in a column called "Vows," and now that I've been on this beat for so long a strange thing has happened: I'm considered an expert on love. Around Valentine's Day every year, television stations from all over the country call, asking me to speak, to shed some light on the subject. But after all this time, love is still mostly a mystery to me. The only thing I can confidently say is this: love is as plentiful as oxygen. You don't have to be perfectly thin, naturally blond, supersuccessful, funny, knowledge-able about politics, socially connected, or even particularly charming to find it. I've interviewed many people who were down on their luck in every way—an artist unable to sell his paintings and living in an illegal loft with leaky plumb-ing; a ballerina with chronic back problems; a physicist who had been on 112 (he counted) disastrous blind dates; a clarinet player who was a single dad and could barely meet the rent payments. But love, when they found it, brought humor, candlelight, fun, adventure, poetry, home-cooked meals, and interesting conversations into their lives.

When people ask me where to find love, I cannot give them any addresses. Instead, I tell a story about one of my first job interviews when I arrived in New York. I inter-viewed for a job at a famous literary magazine, with a leg-endary editor. I had no experience or skills, and he didn't even for one second consider hiring me. But he did give me some advice I will never forget. He said, "Go out into the world. Work hard and concentrate on what you love to do, writing. If you become good, we will find you. It may take five years. It may take ten. But if your work stands out, we will call you."

That's what I tell people looking for love. Don't read ar-ticles about how to trap, ensnare, seduce, or hypnotize a mate. Don't worry about your lipstick or your height, be-cause in the end it's not going to matter. Just live your life well, take care of yourself, and don't mope, complain, or shop too much. Love will find you.

Eventually it even found me. I finally fell in love at

twenty-eight. I met my husband in a stationery store in East Hampton, Long Island, near the Atlantic Ocean. I was buying a typewriter ribbon (it was a long time ago), and he was looking at Filofaxes. I remember that his eyes perfectly matched his faded blue jeans. He remembers that my sneakers were full of sand—he still talks about those sneakers and how they evoked for him the beach, his childhood, bonfires by the ocean, driving on the sand in an old Jeep, all the things he lived for. For us, it didn't take more than a tiny detail, a pair of sand-filled sneakers, the slightest brushstroke, to start love going.

How did I know it was love? Our first real date lasted nine hours. We couldn't stop talking. When I was with him on airplanes, I was so distracted I forgot to be afraid of turbulence. No matter where we were, I never had to run to the ladies' room to calm myself down or think of something to say. I'd never been able to dance in my life, but I could dance with him, perfectly in step, gliding like lovers do. I learned it's love when you finally stop tripping over your toes.

I also knew it was love because we had the strangest things in common. We both believed finding a penny with the head up meant good luck. We were also both afraid to actually pick up lucky pennies. Now, untouchable pennies lie all over our house and we don't have to explain why to each other. We both liked to drive long, long distances, while listening to sad country songs. We were both hippies once. He lived in a tepee in Nova Scotia; I lived in a Volkswagen the color of egg yolk in Colorado.

The best love stories I've heard are ones where two people have the strangest combination of things in common.
Recently, I attended a wedding between a private eye (the
bride) and a kayaking guide (the groom) who both know
the Latin names of nearly every star in the sky, love camping out, go to Catholic church on Sundays, eat at McDon-
ald's, smoke when no one's looking, and listen to Christmas
carols year-round. You have to believe they were meant to
be together.

I've also learned differences can be as romantic, and as
necessary, as similarities. One couple I interviewed, Lois (a
minister) and Hal (a computer scientist), had lots in common—both loved cotton clothes, esoteric movies, mismatched dinnerware, science fiction, ethical debates, the
Grand Canyon, and books on tape. But they were also very
different. She talks nonstop, even with strangers, while he
is quiet and private. She's a beautiful singer; he's tone deaf.

"That's one thing I miss, the two of us singing together,"
Lois said. "But it's okay. You can't have it all. Actually, you
wouldn't want it all in one relationship. If you got it, you'd
live like a mouse in a hole and never come out or make
friends or see the world."

A year after we met, I married my husband in a small,
dainty Victorian church that sits like a conch shell in the
dunes of Southampton, Long Island. Our wedding was a total disaster.

I wore my mother's dress, which didn't fit me well—all
night long it felt like someone was stepping on the hem.
The sleeves were so tight it felt like I was having my blood

pressure taken. I wore a headpiece that was as fragile as a bird's nest and began sliding down my head as soon as I started down the aisle. The minister, a man I didn't know well, spoke at length about menopause, madness, and marriage.

Things only got worse. We held the reception in an old hotel full of Tiffany lamps, curvy velvet couches, and cigar smoke that hung permanently in the air, like smog in L.A. As I entered the hotel, my dress instantly stuck to the floor, which had been polished with a substance as sticky and thick as butterscotch sauce. All night, if I wanted to move at all, I had to lift my train up and carry it in my arms like a bundle of firewood. By the end, I was so depressed I almost ate the entire banana wedding cake.

I learned you can have the worst luck at your wedding, you can even have bad luck throughout your entire life. You can never get asked to dance as a teenager; you can experience hundreds of painfully awkward blind dates; you can look and feel like a bag lady on your wedding day. And still, love can find you and stay with you.

Nearly eight years after we were married, my husband and I had our first child. The thing I now know about love is that if it keeps going, it changes all the time. It reminds me of climbing mountains—the trail is so much longer, more interesting, more difficult, more tiring, and more varied than you ever imagined starting out. Love is one thing at the beginning and something else entirely years later. It winds through so much territory you can't be prepared for, like parenthood, which is the particular forest we're in now.

One couple I recently interviewed got married after eight years of living together and giving birth to two children. "If marriage is about bonding, our marriage took place in the birthing room," the groom said. "Nothing could have tied us together more than having children." For me, having children has been the most educational stop on my journey to figure out love.

Our older son is almost three, and like many toddlers, he takes transitions of all kinds very seriously. For instance, the transition from breakfast to playtime is a huge deal for him, tantamount to moving from the East Coast to the West Coast for an adult. When he leaves a room, he has to somberly say good-bye to every single thing in it. Good-bye, teddy bear. Good-bye, fire truck. Good-bye, books. Good-bye, comfy chair. Watching him reminds me of what it's like to fall in love—everything gains meaning and seems more important, including inanimate things. Chairs and books deserve a good-bye. Even the light improves. At least that's how it was for me.

If love lasts, spending your days with another person does change you. The person you are with alters the food, humor, conversation, people, and sports, in your life. It changes the books you read and how you think about them, the amount of sugar you eat, the walks you take, how often you swim in the ocean.

To promise to see the same person in your kitchen night after night after night is not only a life-altering experience, it's a humbling one. My husband has seen me fall asleep on the couch, with my sweatpants sliding up to my knees. And yet I can still ask him for everything from a loan to a compliment if I really need it. I have heard many definitions of soul mates over the years. One woman described finding hers this way: "I always felt like a fish out of water, and when I met him, he was the same fish." But my own definition of a soul mate is someone who will give you compliments, even when you beg for them, and still mean it.

I always thought falling in love would change me into a more Ralph Laurenesque kind of person. I'd suddenly live in a beautiful log cabin and take walks at night with my five golden retrievers in beautiful powdery snow with mountains in the background. Love did change me a lot, but not the way I expected. Instead of transforming me into a more photogenic, glamorous person, love has made me quiet and given me real peace. I have always been a boisterous, chaotic, and gregarious person, someone who talks so loudly friends hold the phone out at a distance when they're listening to me. As long as I can remember, I've been a shouter.

Consequently, I always imagined I'd have a "loud" life, full of children and friends and touch football games and dogs and gossip sessions that went on until everyone was hoarse. But my husband is quiet, the sort of person who appreciates a fire with one log in it. An architect, he told me on one of our first dates he didn't seek big success or giant money, he just wanted to build a few sturdy houses that fit naturally into the landscape. Now, we live in a small farmhouse with a view of the ocean from the rooftop. We have two children. The four of us read books together at night, cuddled on the couch like kittens. It's so quiet here, I heard the snow falling on frozen leaves the other day. For me, love has changed everything.

When I first started writing about weddings, my main goal was to describe, in the least frilly way possible, very frilly and overdone things—gigantic wedding dresses, million-dollar flower displays, cakes decorated with sugar swans. But as soon as I began receiving mail from readers, I started to realize people do not really care about cake frosting and petticoats. What truly captures their interest—and what has held mine for all these years—are the love stories.

I receive lots of letters begging me for more details on how certain couples met or fell in love or kept love going, but hardly any asking for more details about the center-pieces. One letter writer asked for more information on why a certain couple had waited two years to kiss. Another inquired about two young advertising executives and how they managed to fall in love again after breaking up, burn-ing each other's love letters, and wearing sunglasses to avoid eye contact whenever they met. Still another asked about an investment banker and a scriptwriter who had sur-vived a bicoastal relationship. Some people even requested phone numbers and addresses of people in the column, hoping to have heart-to-heart talks with them.

As for myself, I have come to view "Vows" as a small-town kind of column. I see it as a weekly offering of stories and quotes from neighbors on a subject as familiar and mys-terious as the moon—love. Over the years, I haven't be-come a more hard-bitten, hard-skinned reporter. Just the opposite: Inevitably, every weekend I cry at some point during the ceremony. Tears splash all over my notebook, like quarters dropping.

And once in a while, on the beat, I'll hear a love story that really gives me the goosebumps, one that makes me feel as though I've seen the rare, real thing. In this book, I've collected twelve of those goosebump love stories. Eleven of them come from my years of interviewing, and one of them comes from my own home. All of them explain some aspect of love—how it feels, how it changes you, where it comes from. They are stories with happy endings, all of them, and I write them down here as proof that love, guts, grace, perfect partners, and very good luck do in fact exist. Love, in my opinion, is not a fantasy experience, not the stuff of romance novels or fairy tales. It's as gritty and real as the subway, it comes around just as regularly, and, as long as you can just stick it out on the platform, you won't miss it.

Love
Lessons

The Boy Next

Door

FRIENDS OFTEN ask me what I have learned from my job of crashing weddings full of strangers every week.

I've learned that people are as acutely alert and curious in the presence of a stranger as a herd of deer is. Inevitably, guests stare at me during weddings, wondering what a lonesome-looking woman with a large notebook is doing in their midst. Sometimes, when I approach guests for quotes, they scatter like deer, running just far enough away for safety but continuing to watch me closely. It reinforces my belief that people are definitely members of the animal kingdom.

I've also learned that the world is huge, so much bigger than I ever thought. Week after week, I walk into a roomful of people living in their own insular worlds of high-fashion models or literary types or fast-paced financiers with salaries and frequent flier miles in the seven digits. It's always a different crowd, wedding after wedding. I've learned if your love life falls apart, if you get fired or bored with your circle of friends, there is always hope. There are lots and lots of other universes and interesting corners of the world to explore.

I've also learned that love is a lot like pain—everyone describes it differently and probably everyone experiences it differently, too. Some people have a high tolerance for love and never become overwrought or hysterical about it. They are the ones who don't sit by the phone saying Hail Marys so it will ring. Others feel love intensely—it makes them giddy, shaky, hyperactive, euphoric, senseless. The lesson is, don't compare yourself to others. When love enters your system, you may be as calm as someone in a yoga class, or you may feel totally crazy. It will affect you in its own way.

I've also learned that guts and humor are the most important qualities a person can have when looking for anything from a job to an apartment to love. Use your guts to stick it out until you've found exactly what you want and use your humor to keep from whining too much while you look.

The most important thing I have learned, though, is that disasters, during weddings and in life, are never as disastrous as you think. And perfection is never entirely perfect.

When I was a young girl growing up in Philadelphia, my family was not hugely wealthy, but we were surrounded by very rich neighbors. Because of them, I dreaded the summertime. In the summer, everyone I knew left the city for their summer homes on a lake with a hard-to-spell Indian name, in the Adirondacks or the Poconos or Maine. I remember thinking that our life would be perfect if only we also had a lake to go to, a glassy body of water lying in the woods like a big mirror, surrounded by evergreen trees as tall and pointy as church steeples. We could canoe and sunbathe and skinny-dip. When we had parties on our dock, our laughter would carry across the water like the echoes of firecrackers.

Throughout my entire childhood, I used to moan to my family every summer, "If only we were lake people!"

Now, after years of writing the "Vows" column and listening to love stories from doctors, dentists, poets, investment bankers, rock stars, computer geeks, socialites, and waitresses, I no longer want to be a lake person. I have interviewed so many survivors on this job, people who were living anything but the perfect lake life, and they are the ones I admire most now.

I remember one bride who was marrying for the second time, after having been widowed in her twenties. She was a dress designer who looked like a wilder version of Audrey Hepburn, like Hepburn after several vodkas. This bride drove a broken-down car with windshield wipers that she operated by pulling shoelaces, from *inside* the car. She was accident-prone: Once, soon after moving into a new house, she almost burned it down when she lit a Christmas wreath on fire. "Oh, what a housewarming!" she later joked.

She was also tragedy-prone: Her first husband died

shortly after they were married, of a brain tumor. Still, she laughed all the time. She never made it through a conversation without laughing. At her second wedding, after finding love again, she summed up her view of life this way: "Death is serious. Everything else isn't."

I remember another survivor-bride, a single mother in her fifties who had brought up two daughters alone in a small house. She worked constantly and had no free time, but she never walked outside without her hair looking beautiful, not even on Sunday morning to get the paper. That's the kind of person she was. When her daughters left home for college, she went on a serious, methodical search for love. Although most of her friends thought she was crazy and risking her life, she answered personal ads and met all kinds of men—some insulting and ill-tempered, many balding or wearing loose-fitting toupees, several who drank too much, a few who were unemployed, a lot who were heavier than they admitted on the phone. Most were losers, the sort of people you'd hate to be seated beside on an airplane. But she stuck it out. She even pretended to be interested in sports with her more athletic dates, although she often said her idea of a physical workout was Christmas caroling in an open convertible. She forced herself to stay cheerful, disastrous date after disastrous date, holding her mouth in the shape of a smile sometimes, like a child desperately holding her eyes open so she can stay awake a little longer. Then, after years of fake smiles, she finally met and fell in love with a handsome, impish advertising executive who wore pin-striped shirts, hadn't lost any of his hair, drove a sports car, and had eyes that twinkled like Christmas lights.

I have also met plenty of perfect brides, people with glossy hair that doesn't tangle, who never seem to gain weight, who never have had their hearts broken, who glided into everything from the most prestigious kindergarten to marriage. But I have learned: An easy, pretty life by the lake is lovely, but a difficult life with broken hearts, loneliness, rejection letters, creditors calling, and darkness makes people funnier in the end. In general, perfect brides cry if their dress rips on the floor. Survivor-brides laugh.

Madeline Mingino, my favorite survivor-bride, sent me a fax a few years ago, saying she had a great love story for me. As it turned out, it was hers. Madeline is the sort of person who wears long, flowing velvet dresses, loves overstuffed comfortable couches that you can sink into like a mudbath, never neglects her houseplants, and always has a homemade pie in the kitchen to offer visitors. She hugs her friends a lot and seems driven to cheer others up, the way some people are driven to make money, get thin, or get married. She never loses patience with heart-to-heart talks. The older members of her Long Island family recall that during her christening as a baby, a Good Humor ice cream truck was parked outside the church and its ringing bells could be heard throughout the ceremony. Madeline grew up, they say, to be the sweetest, most good-humored person in the family.

If any of Madeline's friends are going through a hard

time, she is the first to offer recipes, remedies, outings, and distractions. She often bakes them a chocolate dot pumpkin cake—her favorite—or takes them on long, exhausting walks, another specialty. Even as a teenager, brisk walks were her cure for everything from headaches to broken hearts to anxiety attacks.

Tony Giordano, Madeline's best friend and her former high school English teacher, remembers, "One time Madeline saw me in the hallway, and I was very nervous about a school play we were putting on and she asked, 'Are you all right?' Then she took my arm and said, 'Let's take a walk.' We walked out the building and around a very long block, and she just chatted and chatted. When we got back to the school, she said, 'Now, are you going to be okay?'"

When she was twenty-nine, Madeline married a lawyer, and a few years later they moved into a bungalow surrounded by old trees in Flatbush, Brooklyn. Madeline brought to the marriage and new house her usual good cheer, homemade pies, hearty stews, soft down couches, opera records and handsewn bedspreads. The house was often filled with music and the smell of bread baking. She painted the walls inside pale pink and decorated the living room with pink-and-white armchairs and her collection of blue-and-white china. She sewed curtains that let the sunlight in. She called it her storybook cottage. And when her husband returned home from law school, and later from his law firm, they would often sit together on the porch and drink her homemade raspberry-and-rose-petal tea, a concoction she created to soothe him at the end of the day.

She made dozens of homemade teas, ones that cheered people up, gave them more energy, helped bring on sleep, chased away bad thoughts, even one that was supposed to bring love.

"My life seemed perfect," she said. "I had a wonderful house and an excellent husband, a very dedicated, very hardworking, very cheerful husband, a person who always pitched in, a wonderful father. I thought I was so lucky."

In the early years of their marriage, Madeline had two children, started a food co-op with neighbors, and baked chocolate dot pumpkin cakes whenever anyone she knew was feeling sad. If you had asked her about the future then, she would have said she saw herself going back to work as a theater producer after her kids grew up, letting her hair go gray naturally, and never falling out of love with her husband. Her marriage seemed as indestructible to her as the solar system; you couldn't shoot arrows at it, you couldn't pour water on it, you couldn't destroy it even if you wanted to.

Long before her hair turned gray, she and her husband broke up. It happened while they were standing in the kitchen one afternoon. "We were married for thirteen years," Madeline said. "I was thirty-one when my first child, Eli, was born. I was thirty-seven when Thea was born. I was forty when my husband informed me he would be leaving to 'find himself.'" Their marriage ended in about ten minutes. He had already packed his suitcases. From then on, she referred to his departure as "the betrayal."

After the betrayal, she couldn't talk for days. She says it

was a hurricane-force heartbreak, something she didn't think she could possibly survive. "When love stops and you don't expect it to stop, it's so unnatural," she said. "Physically, it was the worst feeling I had ever experienced. After he left, I couldn't put food in my mouth. I had a housekeeper at the time, and she would literally feed me and I would take the food out of my mouth. I was in total shock. I felt like my life had been stolen from me. It was as if someone came in like a thief and took everything."

Although she had always thought of herself as a strong, invincible woman, someone with remedies, cakes, and homemade teas for every misfortune, she had no remedy for this. For days, she stayed in bed, crying. After about a week, she tiptoed out of bed and remembers feeling like Rip Van Winkle, waking up in a world she didn't recognize, the world of a single mother, a woman alone. It suddenly hit her: she had to learn to back the car out of the driveway, organize the bills, work the VCR, sleep by herself. Just thinking about her new life was unbearable—she got right back into bed.

For her, getting over heartbreak was like going through physical therapy—she had to learn how to walk again, to eat again, to live independently all over again. She started with the most basic goal—getting out of bed. Once she did that, she remembered how she used to cure her problems as a teenager and started taking long, long walks. Every day after the kids went to school, Madeline walked for miles around her neighborhood, through city parks and vacant lots, glass crunching under her feet like hard candy, feeling stunned that she was on her own but determined to "rebuild myself like an old house," as she put it. She preferred walking in bad weather, especially heavy rain or severe snowstorms. She relished hail, looked forward to thunderstorms.

"I walked fast and alone; the colder the weather the better it was," she said. "I needed lots of cold air and oxygen. It gave me strength."

On one of her walks, shortly after the betrayal, Madeline ran into her neighbors, Morty and Marion Friedman. Although she didn't know Morty and Marion well, she thought of them as the perfect couple. They were always outside in their front yard, laughing and tending to their wild rambling English garden, handling the flowers as gently as they would handblown glass. A patent lawyer in his fifties, Morty resembled Gandhi in both his slight stature and calm personality. It seemed to Madeline that he was always smiling serenely, like someone who had just taken a sip of great wine.

But Madeline especially loved Marion, who was loud and bawdy and full of life. When Madeline walked by this time, wearing her baggy broken-heart clothes, with tearstains on her cheeks, Marion called out to her, "What the hell is the matter with you?"

Madeline remembers, "I told her what happened and she said very supportive and funny things like, 'Oh, the heck with him!' And, 'If he doesn't appreciate you, let him go.' She made some jokes, she cracked me up so I wasn't crying anymore. Marion was a very attractive woman with a crew cut and unusually long earrings and sweeping, colorful clothing. She was just a lovable oddball. She always cheered me up."

Madeline often passed Morty and Marion over the next few years, as she walked and walked and walked around the neighborhood, up and down hills, in lightning, pouring rain, freezing temperatures, and stinging winds. "When my marriage ended, I felt ramshackle," Madeline said. "I felt in pieces. I said to myself, You're shattered and little by little you'll put it back together. And I did put it back together, not only by walking but by enjoying small, everyday things—sewing, sunshine, cleaning the house, music. I listened to opera, rock 'n' roll, and the blues. All three of those musical forms have passion, and passion gives you strength. I went to movies and museums. Beauty is essential for recovery. I never went to singles bars or drank alcohol or did anything I considered dark or negative."

About five years after the betrayal, Madeline turned on the radio, and while she was listening to a religious talk show, she realized she had almost rebuilt herself. "There was a minister giving a one-minute sermon," she remembered. "He said we are all pilgrims, and sometimes as pilgrims, in the course of our journey, we find ourselves in a wilderness. And the way to find your way out is to look for familiar landmarks. For me, my familiar landmark was cooking. We'd been living on take-out food since my husband left—my kitchen was covered with dust. I remember standing in the kitchen soon after that, and I cleaned it up, mopped the place, and started cooking again. That was one of my familiar landmarks, cooking for my children. And before long, I was out of the wilderness."

Nearly six years after her husband left, Madeline called a friend and told him she was finally okay. She did not expect to fall in love ever again, she said, but for the first time since the betrayal, she could see the future and even picture herself as a grandmother—gray-haired, feisty, independent, self-sufficient, making chocolate pumpkin dot cakes for friends in trouble.

Soon after that, on one of her walks through the neighborhood, she ran into Morty Friedman alone in his front yard, pruning roses. He did not seem to be his usual serene, peaceful self; instead, his face was creased like a letter that had been read over and over again. Almost echoing Marion's words of several years before, Madeline said, "What the hell happened to you, Morty?"

As it turned out, Marion had died a few weeks before, so suddenly that all her favorite belongings—her purple and turquoise long dresses, the Fiesta ware she collected, dishes as colorful as Lifesavers—were still strewn all over the house, like flower petals.

Remembering how Marion had always cheered her up, joking and laughing while her earrings jangled like wind chimes, and remembering the sickening feeling of her own heartbreak, Madeline invited Morty on one of her long walks. She insisted he come, just once. Maybe, *hopefully*, the weather would be horrible, she said. Rainstorms are as soothing as chamomile tea for someone with a broken heart, she told him. Walking in a snowstorm is like seeing a bride appear at the end of an aisle—it whitens your world and obscures the dark side of things, for a little while.

Okay, he said.

As it turned out, it was a sunny day when Madeline and Morty took their first walk together. And for the first time in many years, she was the stronger person present, the one not weeping.

"We walked through Prospect Park in Brooklyn, and she described her experiences and I described mine," Morty remembers. "Even though they were totally dissimilar, there was pain associated with both, and we just soothed one another."

After his wife died, Morty said, he felt as if he were dying also. He couldn't sleep. He lost his appetite. He felt as solitary as someone on a deathbed. "I discovered very quickly that I didn't like to be by myself," he said. "One night, I went alone to a local bar and restaurant, and everyone was eating with someone else and I actually started to cry. I felt so lonely and out of place. I don't know how it is for other people, but I can't live a full life by myself. It's hard to imagine what I would be like if I didn't have love. I had a small taste of it, and it was very unpleasant."

A few days after their first walk, Madeline dropped off a chocolate dot pumpkin cake at Morty's house, on an expensive blue hand-painted plate with yellow daisies around the rim. "I remember when she left and I had the cake in my hands, I thought, Oh, great, it's on a plate that has to be returned," Morty said.

Before long, Morty and Madeline started walking together regularly and talking about everything from loneliness to opera to the Beatles to the fact that they were beginning to think about each other all the time. After only a few grueling walks together, Morty began to feel Madeline was always around, a perfume that never faded. "Our relationship quickly became intense," he said. "I felt like we were married after a couple of weeks."

Before Madeline, Morty imagined that finding love as a widower would be like solving an impossible algebraic equation, a combining of two long, complex, hard-to-understand adult lives. But to his surprise, there was an elementary ease to being with Madeline—it required no torturous late-night talks, no long entries in his journal, no weighing of the pros and cons, almost no thought. It seemed to Morty that Madeline could enter his life and home as naturally and easily as air though an open window.

Only six weeks after they began walking together, Morty bought Madeline a gift: a country house in her hometown of Bellport, Long Island, around the corner from the church where she was christened to the music of a Good Humor truck parked outside. The house he chose was a white, pristine, nineteenth-century farmhouse with low beamed ceilings, old wooden floors the color of strong tea, lots of fireplaces, and a staircase that creaked like a boat in stormy weather whenever someone climbed it. After Morty gave her the house, Madeline recalls, "I stood on the lawn and wept. I never thought I would fall in love again."

During their first summer in the house, they transplanted

the wild rambling English garden Morty and Marion had planted to their backyard in Bellport. Sitting in the window seat of their kitchen now, they can see the peach-colored roses Morty and Marion planted together, next to fuchsia ones with petals as ruffled as a tuxedo shirt, next to high wheat-colored grasses. "We call it our miniature *Howard's End*," Madeline says.

In the kitchen, they replaced the wooden cabinets with glass ones and filled them with the Fiesta ware Marion collected during years and years of scouring flea markets and yard sales—cake platters, water pitchers, coffee cups as colorful as she was. While some people might think living among Marion's things would be eerie for Madeline, and unbearably sad for Morty, they both love showing off her favorite finds to visitors. Even when they're alone in the kitchen, they say they enjoy her bright presence.

"Morty and I have started a new life, but I don't feel we need to erase Marion's memory," Madeline says. "Marion was a fun and wonderful and kooky person, a bohemian kind of gal. I saved her linens and I use them all. There are times when I say, 'Oh, thank you, Marion, this is so beautiful.'"

Madeline and Morty also collect paintings and sculptures of angels—a statue of a cherub with rosy cheeks, curly blond hair, and powerful wings now looks down from a ledge above their front door, greeting visitors. Some of their teacups are also decorated with angels; while having tea at their house, you'll look down at your cup and see a little painted angel on the bottom, lying there like a lucky penny. In every way their house feels full of good luck. On a recent visit, Madeline brought out a chocolate dot pumpkin cake and shyly said they wanted to show me one more thing—their unusually large collection of four-leaf clovers, most of them found in the backyard. Each one is mounted, framed, and dated. Several were found on the same day. A few are enormous, as big as daisies. Madeline and Morton hold their large pile of clovers lovingly, then return them to the living room wall, where they hang among family photos. Morty has even found a few four-leaf clovers on their walks through Brooklyn, growing in cracks in the pavement. "It's ridiculous how many he finds," said Madeline. "It's like finding a needle in a haystack."

To Tony Giordano, the bride's old high school teacher, it makes perfect sense that Madeline and Morty would find four-leaf clovers as easily as other people spot dandelions. "I'm a cynic," Tony said. "I've seen lots of partnerships and I've supported some, but I've been frightened for most. But Morty and Madeline have magic."

Exactly one year after they met, Morty and Madeline were married in their Bellport house. The wedding took place in December, and their living room was decorated with poinsettias the color of faded pink Bermuda shorts. There was a swarm of tiny white Christmas lights on the fireplace, glowing like fireflies, and two Christmas trees, one covered with paper angels. Outside the house, it appeared something very unusual was going on—the lawn was the only *white* one on the street. Before the ceremony, the bride had poured fake snow all over the grass as a way of reminding everyone that this wedding was unbelievable and miraculous, that she once thought she had about as much chance of remarrying as there is of snow falling heavily on only one lawn in town. Also, she wanted guests to hike through snow to the house, as a reminder of how much she and Morty love to walk in snowstorms.

When asked about their plans for the future, Morty said, "Someday we'll retire, although we can't conceive of ourselves retiring so the word *retirement* means we'll be doing something different, just not working nine to five. We might be working eight to six, seven days a week."

A year later, when I last spoke to Morty and Madeline, they had retired. She had turned fifty; he had entered his sixties. For the first time in years, Madeline wasn't working. Instead, she spent her days reading books, sunk down deep in one of her many comfortable couches, listening to opera, watching soup on the stove, and hanging eucalyptus leaves from her chandeliers (something she does year-round). Morty spends his days more or less the same way—gardening, reading, thinking, and sitting perfectly still. They are people who have found peace; you can even hear it when talking to them on the telephone.

During one of our interviews, I asked Madeline to tell me her philosophy of love—what was her explanation for why she found Morty? Was it because of angels, because of four-leaf clovers, because they are simply very blessed and lucky people? No, she said, that's not why.

This, according to Madeline, is the explanation: Recently she visited a psychic, mainly because she wanted to try to speak to Marion. Madeline had never seen a psychic before, and she laughed as she recounted her awkward, nervous visit, feeling like she had finally, totally lost her mind. "I really wanted to get in touch with Marion," Madeline said. "I felt worried about things, like selling Morty's house and getting rid of things. I didn't want to be the other wife who came along and dismantled everything. I'm not the kind of person who says, 'Oh, well, she's dead. Everything's over.' But apparently Marion is okay with everything. She was happy for us. I always felt I was chosen because of how everything happened so quickly with Morty, how we fell in love so fast. And through the psychic, Marion told me, 'I needed someone for him, and I chose you.'"

Soul Mates

On-line

THE BEST THING about writing "Vows" is that faxes pile up like snowdrifts in my office. And they aren't ordinary faxes at all. In the middle of the day, or even in the middle of the night, people hoping to be in the column send me their love stories. It makes my house seem magical, a place where tales of couples meeting on the sidewalk or in the cat food aisle of the supermarket arrive as regularly as airplanes at Kennedy Airport. I never get used to the faxes, or bored by them. Every time an airplane actually lands, it seems miraculous to me. And anytime I hear about someone falling in love, I have the same feeling.

Of all the tales that pile up in my office, my favorites are the ones about love on-line. Even though Internet courtships are as common as blind dates these days, I still think there is something otherworldly about couples who meet on-line. They remind me of test-tube babies. Someone appears in your life one day, nothing but a sentence on your computer screen, maybe even a partial sentence, an embryo, and eventually grows into your real-life, flesh-and-blood soul mate.

While high tech, the on-line world is not cold. I think in some ways it's as romantic as a dark lover's lane. Looks don't matter since you can't see each other. Geography isn't an issue—I once interviewed a couple who met via the Internet when he was living in a tent in the Amazon rain forest and she in a tiny Manhattan apartment.

But the best thing about falling in love on-line is that it's so easy to express exactly how you feel. If you're crazy about someone, you can e-mail them in the middle of the night. If you tire of an on-line admirer, you can delete the whole relationship instantly. On the Internet, the heart rules.

Two years ago, I received a fax from a bride named Tse-Feng Susan Chang, who calls herself Susie. She was about to marry a guy she met on-line, but she began her letter by admitting that she had never had much luck when it came to men.

She had recently broken up with a longtime boyfriend and swore she would never go out with another man named Peter again. "From high school on, I'd dated a long succession of tall, depressed men named Peter, and he was the last," she said.

At the time, Susie was twenty-seven and lived with one cat and hundreds of books in the Hell's Kitchen neighborhood of New York City, in a tiny fifth-floor apartment. After she broke up with the last Peter, she often ate dinner alone on the old rooftop of her building, which was as soft and lumpy as an old pillow. Up there, she sometimes blared music and danced alone, attracting waves from passersby on the sidewalk below. Over time, she concluded she had about as much chance of finding long-lasting love in New York as she did of finding a starfish in the Hudson River.

"I was starting to feel skeptical, like if there's someone out there, what are the chances I could find him?" she said. "My diary at the time is filled with curious ruminations about odds and probability."

If you saw her from afar, you might think Susie was a ballerina. She's petite, slim, graceful, and as delicate looking as a blown-glass figurine, yet her personality is as strong and forceful as a kickboxer's. Susie is full of those kinds of contradictions. On one hand, she's an academic and disciplined person whose posture is perfect and whose clothes are rarely wrinkled. She graduated from Harvard in three years, works as a book editor at Oxford University Press, and considers poetry in ancient Greek to be good beach reading. On the other hand, she's a free-spirited bohemian who owns several decks of tarot cards, consults astrologers, believes in crystal balls, and does the tango alone on rooftops.

As a child growing up in Dobbs Ferry, New York, she practiced the piano for five hours a day, under the strict supervision of her mother. "Pu was the last name of my mother's side of the family, and there's this unbelievable Pu work ethic," she said. "Everyone is trying to improve themselves in some obvious way. It's not unusual to see my cousins sitting there on an aerobics bicycle, eating granola, and watching a language video. That's very Pu."

Still, as a child, she spent most of her free time looking out her bedroom window at the Hudson River and daydreaming. That's very Susie.

"She was always a dreamer when she was a kid," said Pang-Mei Chang, her cousin. "We'd say, 'Susie, wake up!' She used to tell people, 'Hi, my name is Susie Chang, and from my window, I can see the Hudson River.'"

After Susie broke up with the last Peter and decided she would probably never find true love, she did not sit around and mope. Instead, in an effort to cheer herself up, she started saxophone lessons, planted aromatic herbs and spices in her windowbox, and traveled to the Virgin Islands, where she learned how to scuba dive, and ended up having an affair with a stranger she met on the beach. She also threw herself into ballroom dancing, which took the place of real love in her life for a while.

"I was an editor by day, ballroom dancer by night," she said. "You walk into a studio and there's hundreds of people of every race, age, and profession—there are single mothers, a lot of computer people, mathematicians, people who love Fred and Ginger movies. You never know your partner's last name, and in fact you may not know their first name. They just walk up to you and say, 'Waltz?'"

She bought rhinestone dancing shoes that sparkled in her closet like miniature disco balls and the sort of slinky gowns movie stars used to wear while walking poodles or sitting by swimming pools in the 1920s. Friends nicknamed her The Super Waltz Girl. Whenever she traveled on business, she would look up dance studios in the yellow pages and spend the evening doing the merengue or salsa with strangers in unfamiliar towns. But after a while, even though she had a partner every night, she started leaving the studios feeling lonelier than ever.

"Ballroom dancing provides you with an outlet for your energy, and it's a wonderful, dramatic, exciting form, but it leaves you dangling in the end," she said. "You've flung yourself into this incredibly passionate environment and worked yourself up to this feverish pitch, and then you go home alone to your cat."

So one night, sitting at home with her cat, Susie decided to take a shot in the dark: she placed a long, poetic ad in the personals section of Yahoo! on the Internet. As if she had screamed "Hello?" into the Grand Canyon or tossed a message-in-a-bottle into the ocean, she didn't actually expect a response. "Like so many women here in New York, I'd given up my expectations of finding anyone," she said. "Posting an ad was really just a way to tempt fate."

In a way, putting an ad on-line was a high-tech version of ballroom dancing. "Like ballroom dancing, placing an ad on-line is kind of random," she said. "You throw yourself out there, and you never know what you're going to get."

Susie's ad, like her dancing, was full of grace and beauty, but there was also some sadness showing underneath, like a slip that's visible when it shouldn't be. It read, "I'm a young woman with an old soul; I like the hot sun and the city lights, the glamour of the ballroom, and the silence of the book shelf. I know the difference between anise and dill, among other things, and I *almost* know what fenugreek is. I believe in Manhattan without therapy, the contagiousness of joy and the basic sweetness of life. Often nice things happen to me—strangers give me roses, butchers give me discounts . . . the unwary sometimes fork over their hearts. Some things I have but don't use as much as I maybe should are crayons, a passport, perfect pitch, a blowtorch, reading knowledge of Aeolic, and common sense. I have one cat, no god and three things I prize: kindness, grace and brains. I'm looking for someone who's made the most out of what came in the box: a man with a big and open heart and a big and open mind and a strong body that's graceful at rest and in motion. Handsome sadists, dim Adonises and brilliant couch potatoes are fine in principle but not for me. That's the big picture—if it seems right to you, drop a line and the specifics will follow."

Very quickly, within minutes after she clicked Submit and sent the ad, she began receiving replies. Over the next several days, whenever she turned on her computer, she had e-mail waiting, like strangers lined up outside her door. "As a kid, I loved to be the first to get the mail," she said. "You'd hear the creak of the lid on the mailbox and just go running out to see what you got. It was the same way with my Yahoo! mailbox. I would go into Yahoo! and it'd say three new messages or sixteen new messages, and it was just this feeling of, What's in store for me today? It could be a stalker who's going to kill me, or it could be my future husband. I loved the mystery of not knowing what's coming."

She heard from a photographer, an investment banker, a pediatrician, an ex–baseball player, a cook from the Metropolitan Museum, a puppeteer, a ballet dancer, *two* Lufthansa pilots, a registered nurse, and a neurobiologist. Sometimes while walking down a street or sitting in a café, she would watch passerbys and think, Is that the pilot who wrote a long poem, or the ballet dancer who seemed so depressed? For Susie, the process of placing an ad on the Internet made all strangers seem less strange, as if they could be people she'd met on-line who had told her everything about their childhoods, broken hearts, favorite movies, and worst fears. It made her more sympathetic to strangers everywhere—in the grocery store checkout lines, in bookstores and coffee shops, on her way to the office.

"I walk to work every day, and I primarily see people as obstacles," she said. "They're just something you have to get around. It's hard to believe that all those people out there each carry within them this complete and entire world. But when you place an ad, what you get back is a totally random sampling of the interior worlds of a bunch of people. It was so interesting."

In all, over 100 people replied to Susie's ad. "There were some complete sex maniacs," she said. "There were some nice, normal people. There was more than one businessman who was in town for the weekend and logged in from their

hotel room. None were quite right. It was like Goldi-
locks—too hot, too cold."

Finally, she received one response that was perfectly
right. "At first I got this shiver, and then I read it over and
over again," she said.

It was from Randall Dean te Velde, a computer whiz who
is almost ten years older than Susie and, like her, full of
contradictions. He looks like a football-playing frat
brother, yet he's quiet and thoughtful, the sort of guy who
carries around books of poetry and Tibetan Buddhism in his
backpack. He's not as talkative as Susie, but he's equally optimistic and determined to be good-natured. He smiles at
strangers on the street and, like her, believes in Manhattan
without therapy and in the importance of kindness, grace,
and brains. Both are whimsical and sometimes make large,
hard-to-follow leaps of thought between one sentence and
another. They speak in a style that's poetic and awe-
inspiring; you notice it instantly, the way you notice ballet
dancers walking through a crowd. And just as ballet
dancers make you want to improve your posture, Randy
and Susie make you want to improve your vocabulary.

His first reply read, "Your post seemed far too interesting
to pass up. I'd enjoy starting a correspondence with you although my qualifications don't come close to meeting your
demands. I haven't met very many who have even sorted
out their box let alone made the most of its contents. Mine
is in astonishing disarray but I keep hope alive."

When she asked, later in their correspondence, why he

had responded to her ad, Randy told her, "Looking at the ad, I thought, here is somebody—'the contagiousness of joy . . . butchers give me discounts'—I should at least wave and acknowledge her, like old friends trapped on opposite sides of a subway car during rush-hour commute."

At the end of his first e-mail, Randy left his phone number, which Susie called right away just to listen to his voice on the answering machine. A few hours later, she sent him a message. "Your voice is deeper than I expected," she wrote. "Can you see the FDR Drive from your apartment? Do you smoke cigars at the Havana Tea Room? Have you tangoed at the Y?"

She added, "An e-mail correspondence would be delightful. A few more facts to add to the jar: I read for a living though I'm legally blind. I live at the top of 66 stairs, which I sometimes count but more often treat as percussion (*The Rite of Spring* works O.K.). I like macaroons but not macaroni and I always, always mean well."

The two soon became on-line friends, confidants who had never seen each other but told each other almost everything about themselves. "Every day we would start a conversation and talk about things on our mind," she said. "We would share our dreams, ask each other questions. It was so great to have someone to share all your thoughts with, someone you didn't even know. We likened it to having someone to confide in behind a dark screen."

Reading their early correspondence, you can watch them falling in love e-mail by e-mail. Their conversations were full of free associations, whimsical digressions, thoughtful confessions, and quick word plays. There was a genuine connection building sentence by sentence, thread by thread, as if they were knitting a sweater. You can see how well they understand each other's jokes, obscure references, insecurities, philosophies, worries, and worldviews. Reading their letters, it seems that one explanation of love is simply that it's a great conversation. You fall in love with the person whose stories you love listening to, the one who brings out the best stories in you, the one you could talk to driving across the country and back and never be bored. Whenever I interview brides and grooms about their first dates, one thing they tell me over and over is, "Our first date lasted fifteen hours" or "We talked all night, we couldn't stop." The feeling of early love, for many people, is often simply the feeling of wanting to say much, much more.

In their first e-mails, Randy and Susie talked about everything from their current romantic interests to Buddhism, the weather, ballroom dancing, and growing tomatoes. She told him how she tends to wear too much jewelry when she goes to salsa clubs, setting off the metal detectors as she walks in. He described his longtime, live-in girlfriend and how her growing distance startled him more and more each day. She wrote about her beloved rooftop: "My roof, which I coated with SilverKoate Aluminum Roof Coating (for the heat) last weekend, is where I play the saxophone and watch too many sunsets for my own cynical heart."

He wrote to her about his love of cigars and gardening: "So far my work in the garden has only been pruning, hardly a green thumb. My girlfriend (June, by the way) has done all the planting and watering—some herbs and toma-toes in a small patch not in the shade of a large maple. I just made the patch a little bigger by cutting some low-hanging branches."

She replied: "I couldn't help reflecting on the pang that I wished I had a cigar-smoking friend with a garden where I could sit and drink dry vermouth on the rocks and specu-late as to the origin, and necessity, of mosquitoes or bicycle cops or what have you." She told him her idea of a dream job: "My greatest unfulfilled ambition in life is to be a real-life restaurant reviewer. There—you will end by prying all my secrets from me, like sweet peas from a pod."

Over the weeks, they exchanged many secrets but never, ever spoke about meeting in person. Susie, who says she fell in love with Randy after the third e-mail, gradually began to drop hints that they might meet. Randy, by then in the middle of breaking up with his girlfriend, didn't seem to like the idea at all. He wrote to Susie, "I ask you, wouldn't it be a lot better to be disembodied at a time like this? . . . Would you really want to put up with the emotional up-heaval of a breakup as a third-party participant? I think it would be better to sit this one out with a bottle of cham-pagne, burgundy, or a julep or two."

Then he wrote the kind of sentence that would have sent me up to the rooftop with martinis and my saddest CDs if I were Susie. It read, "If your heart is set on locating a soul mate, why not invest in more promising prospects?"

Right after that, though, he added, "But I do enjoy your messages so. If you still want to write, I assure you that you won't find a more appreciative audience."

So they continued to write, and while they ceased speaking of meeting in person, they did exchange physical proof of each other's existence. At one point, he asked her to send him a little token of herself. "He said, 'Why not enclose some sign of you, a shopping list, a page from the notepad by your telephone, something magneted to your refrigerator?'" Susie recalls. After much thought, she sent him a limerick she wrote when she was eight, a cutting of peppermint from her windowbox garden, and a reading of his tarot cards.

"That was the first evidence I had that there was a real person on the other end," Randy said.

A month after their e-mails began, Randy still wanted to remain a "disembodied" correspondent, but Susie was determined to meet him in person. "I wasn't even able to sleep at this point," she said. "I was convinced I'd never meet anyone like him again. Around that time, I had to go on a business trip, and traveling makes you think. I did my work and played my sax by a lake, and I thought and thought and thought. Finally, I made up my mind to meet him."

She didn't tell him about her plan, though. Instead, as she puts it, she "stalked" him. From their conversations, she knew he took a course in TriBeCa on Tibetan Buddhism, so she found out the time of the class and slipped in one evening to search for him. It was like trying to find someone based on his driver's license alone. She didn't know anything about what he looked like except his height, his weight, and his eye color—hazel.

"The July heat was overpowering and the incense was going to my head, but I struggled to find my invisible confidant," she remembers. "After an hour of staring at the backs of fifty men's heads and passing notes to the girl next to me to see if she knew a Randy (she didn't), I finally took my best guess."

The man she thought might be him carried a backpack full of books and had a football player's build and hazel eyes. "I just put my two feet down right in front of him and asked, 'What's your name?'" she recalls. "His eyebrows shot up over his glasses and he said, 'Randy.' And I said, 'Oh, I'm Susie.'"

It took him a while to figure out who "Susie" was. But when he did, he was stunned. "I was shocked at how beautiful she was," he remembered. "I thought she was a fantastic correspondent up to that point, but I had prevented myself from considering her as a romantic possibility. I didn't want to be disappointed if she turned out to be very much of a librarian sort. I love to hike and go scuba diving, and I couldn't imagine being with someone whose life was in books."

That night, they walked around TriBeCa, stopping for a beer here and there and reading Pablo Neruda poetry and tarot cards together. "It emerged that he, like me, was a ballroom-dancing, saxophone-playing ex-classicist," she said. "But to be honest he could have been a cattle-ranching, saber-wielding ex-detective. The connection had already been forged."

In person, their conversations were as easy as they were on-line. "Walking around with him, there was a feeling of complete transparency between us, like there was no barrier between what I was saying and what he was understanding," she said. "There was no explanation necessary. But I really didn't know if he'd want to see me again. I had a sense of dread—I thought, I've just gone and stalked him. I don't think there's any reason he'll be interested in return."

But he was very, very interested. By the time she got home that night, she had an e-mail from him waiting in her mailbox.

After that, they were no longer disembodied correspondents. In August, a month after they had met physically, he moved into her apartment, and before long they could be seen by pedestrians, eating or dancing together on the rooftop. Exactly one year after their e-mail romance began, they were married in Brooklyn aboard *Bargemusic*, a wooden barge that looks like a log cabin floating under the Brooklyn Bridge. On the day of their wedding, the sky was as gray as an old Macintosh computer, which was appropriate—among the guests there were many long-haired computer whizzes (friends of Randy), several of whom had experienced failed, disappointing, and strange on-line romances and shook their ponytails at Randy's luck.

There were also a lot of lithe, beautifully dressed ballroom dancers (friends of Susie). One, Nina Gellert, said she was looking for love but felt too chicken to place a personal ad anywhere, and especially on-line. The mystery, the sense that everyone on-line is wearing a mask, was too spooky for her, too much like Venice at carnival time.

"Just as you bare your soul on the Internet, you bare your body in ballroom dancing," Nina said. "I'll do the ballroom but I won't do the Internet. With ballroom you can see face-to-face who it is. On the Internet some person could be writing saying they're a guy and it turns out they're a thirteen-year-old girl."

While I see couples who meet on-line as otherworldly creatures brought together by some high-tech genie, by the Internet's equivalent of fate and destiny, Susie and Randy don't view themselves that way at all. They say they do not try to explain what brought them together—in their opinion, it wasn't fate, technology, destiny, magic, or even the random coincidence of being on the same website at the same time. They say that many things are impossible to explain—God, musical ability, the disappearance of dinosaurs, clear-air turbulence—and love is among them.

So at their wedding, Susie and Randy asked a friend to read a Pablo Neruda poem about mystery and things that cannot be understood or explained. The poem was essentially a list of impossible questions like, "Where does the lizard buy fresh paint for his tail?" and "Why is the scorpion venomous and the elephant benign?" and "Where do birds die and why are leaves green?"

Finally, Neruda wrote: "What we know comes to so little."

Cloudland

AT EVERY WEDDING, I wonder the same thing—will this love last? No one assumes it will anymore. In fact, some people believe that love can die as quickly as a wildflower picked from the side of the road. It can disappear like a piece of jewelry down the sink drain. You can wrack your brain imagining where it went; you can even use a chainsaw on your plumbing pipes. But a lot of people believe you probably won't find a way to get love back once it's gone.

I've begun to think you can get it back. While writing "Vows," I've interviewed so many couples whose relationships at one time or another seemed as impossible as electrical engineering. I met one bride and bridegroom who were married and divorced in their early twenties. After an argument one night, she ran out of their apartment with an armful of possessions, including her wedding dress and her cat, which she later renamed Divo, short for divorce. For the next fifteen years, they lived in the same neighborhood but avoided each other as assiduously as some people avoid weight gain. Then, one night, feeling lonely, nostalgic, and bold, she called and left a message on his answering machine. Feeling lonely and curious, he called back, and when they got together a few nights later, they spent the evening looking at old photographs of their early married days—dinner parties they threw, their first beach house, a cross-country trip. Within weeks, they were in love again.

Another couple I met had broken up dozens of times. He even moved to California once to avoid her. They both incinerated each other's love letters on several occasions. But still, they eventually fell back in love for good. At their wedding, the bridegroom said, "If you break something and use Superglue on it, it's actually stronger. Scar tissue's tough."

Of all the couples I've interviewed, none are more Superglued together than my own parents. They have been married almost fifty years, but the middle of their marriage was so rough, I remember it as one long argument. They fought almost constantly. They threw telephones, tennis balls, dictionaries, sneakers, and hoagies at each other. I can still hear them arguing, the way you can always hear the ocean if you live near it long enough, even if you move far away.

From my parents, I learned my favorite lesson about love—it returns. Here is their story.

My father calls my mother Lo-Lo, short for Lois. He met her on the steps outside a college dance in 1948 when she walked up to him and asked for a cigarette. My father soon learned she wasn't afraid of much and nothing stopped her from having a good time. If a friend was in the hospital, she'd sneak in bottles of champagne or gin, whatever the friend drank, with little plastic cups and matching napkins. She could swim for miles in the ocean. She loved to ride horses bareback. In the days after they met, my father was taken by my mother the way you're taken by an undertow.

They were opposites in many ways. He grew up in a big Irish Catholic family in Philadelphia, in a row house filled with aunts, sisters, and brothers, friends of the family who were down on their luck, uncles who were priests. The house was like an Irish bar, with everyone gathered around the kitchen table at night, telling stories that went on forever like winding back roads. The rule was, "Survival of the Loudest." My father still loves to sit at the kitchen table late at night, talking. He cries easily. My mother never, ever cries.

She grew up in a Tudor mansion outside New York City, one of five children who learned to waltz, ride horses, quote poetry, and speak intelligently about everything from Renaissance painting to Queen Anne furniture. Her home life, unlike his, was formal and not at all boisterous. Her parents ate dinner in one room, their forks clinking lonesomely against china, while the children ate down the hall. After my mother turned sixteen, her parents occasionally invited her to join them for cocktails, and she was expected to drink bourbon without wincing. She had no problem.

My grandfather stopped working early in life, in his fifties, and my mother's family lived on inheritance and good manners after that. When the inherited money dwindled, they paid their bills with Oriental rugs, grandfather clocks, and pieces of Cloudland. Cloudland was an enormous family farm in Vermont. It was such a high piece of property, my mother said, clouds sometimes skidded across the grass or got caught in tree branches like ghostly birds. Eventually, Cloudland was sold off entirely.

Early in their marriage, I'm told, my mother and father were madly in love. He thought she looked like Ingrid Bergman; she was crazy about his Cary Grant–like looks, his dark, curly hair and green eyes, and the fact that he always won at tennis and football. He had been a football star at Harvard, and pictures of him making touchdowns decorated their first home.

I also know they had an incredible amount of fun early in their marriage. They drove a blue convertible; wore crazy sunglasses; built enormous, hilarious snowmen in the wintertime and dressed them in my mother's fur coats; threw toboggan and tailgate parties; and always asked to eat at the bar in restaurants because they loved talking to strangers. They were never the kind of couple who chose a table by themselves in order to stare into each other's eyes and cuddle and coo. Instead, they found romance in storytelling or driving around in their convertible on beautiful evenings, breaking into the country club pool in the middle of the night, or sledding down mountains holding on to each other for dear life.

As a young couple, they liked to spend weekends in Smithville, New Jersey, with my mother's two great-aunts, Hilda and Veronis. Both spinsters, they lived together in a big house where they never opened the windows. When my parents visited them, they would all sit out on the porch, surrounded by weeping willow trees, and talk about literature while the trees shook in the wind, rustling like wedding dresses.

Soon, my parents had three children, and for a long time, my mother said, she was so happy she was afraid she was going to die and miss out on the fun. When I was about eight, we were driving in her huge station wagon when she suddenly pulled over on the side of the road, screaming that she was having a heart attack. She was about thirty-five at the time and in perfect health. But my younger sister, my brother, and I had to get out of the car and wait on the grass for what seemed like our entire childhoods. Finally, my mother popped up and said, "False alarm!"

I have heard people say love is like wine—some people become dizzy from it, some euphoric, some sweaty and anxious, but inevitably, the first feelings fade.

For my parents, love began to fade when I was about twelve, partly for financial reasons. My father lost money as easily as other people lose paper clips. He had a small law office in Philadelphia, and because he liked good stories better than anything else, he represented clients with great tales—murderers who never intended to murder, a man whose wife disappeared from a golf course one weekend, like a ball shot out of range. But my father's clients rarely had any money to pay him. He once represented a man who owned a Chinese restaurant and for months afterward, we'd come home and our vestibule would be filled with little white cartons of Chinese food, his form of payment. During those years, my mother's mantra became, "The honeymoon is over."

Dad had about as much luck with the stock market as he did with his law practice. It was one financial loss after another, although he turned every one into an hilarious story. He became a part owner of a coal mine that collapsed, literally. He invested in a chain of coffee shops as desolate as diners in Edward Hopper paintings. He invested in sports drinks that no one ever drank.

My parents stopped driving convertibles and started driving the cheapest cars they could find. For years, we traveled in a tiny turquoise Honda that dragged on the street if more than three people rode in it. Most of the old fun left my parents' life. Their toboggan sat in the basement, warping. They fought at night about bills, leaks, tuition, termites. My mother would ask my father to do the dishes, and he'd respond by throwing every pot, pan, plate, and fork into the trash can. They were like two people who had taken the wrong exit off a highway and ended up in a scary neighborhood, arguing hysterically about how to get out of there and back to the right road.

My sister, brother, and I each reacted to their rocky marriage differently. I became a hippie, decorated my room with posters of long-haired motorcyclists, and talked of jumping freight trains across Canada. My brother became a straight-A student and an ice hockey star, while my sister mused day and night about how she was really a princess who had been dropped off accidentally at our house and was awaiting the return of her royal, well-behaved, much more nicely dressed parents.

For years, our parents must have mentioned divorce every day. During most of that time, my mother kept an open suitcase in her room. She'd occasionally throw a few clothes into it, snap it shut, and run out the door, screaming, "Good-bye! I wish I'd left a lot earlier!" to all of us. I remember looking out the windows for her return, the way I now look out airplane windows during a storm to see if there's a break in the clouds or any sign of safe weather ahead.

As it turned out, there was only more turbulence ahead for my parents. They were great at parenting—my mother threw the best birthday parties in our neighborhood, with six-foot-tall cakes and huge fireworks she bought illegally and set off in our backyard like rockets to the moon. But my parents did not seem in love. If anything, it seemed as if their marriage had driven them crazy. My mother gardened too much, late into the night. I'd leave for school in the morning and find cocktail glasses underneath the rose bushes or the tomato vines, glinting in the sun like bracelets. My father continued to take clients who paid him in their own currencies. At night, he listened to Johnny

Cash records over and over again, sometimes slowing the records down so he could hear all the words and sad stories perfectly clearly. During those years, it was as if we were all in a wild ocean, holding on to whatever lifeboats we could find.

After my brother, sister, and I all left for college, we didn't know if Mom and Dad would stay together. Their house seemed to slide into sadness, with our old bedrooms becoming more and more forlorn every year, filled with cast-off tennis trophies, fading diplomas, and shoes no one would ever wear again. For a while, I'd call home and Mom would say Dad was off on "one of his disappearances." He'd go out driving in his car, which he had nicknamed Bermuda, because its heating system billowed out warm, tropical air. In the winter, my mother kept the temperature in the house very cold—she said heat made her sleepy—so Dad spent a lot of time out in Bermuda.

A few years after we all left, my parents decided to renovate the house, beginning with the kitchen. They tore out the lime green sink from 1920, where they had fought so many times over who would wash the dishes. They ripped out the pantry, where my mother kept her gardening tools and where she used to rest after their fights. I can still see her sitting in the little folding beach chair she kept in there, pouring herself a bourbon. I visited her in the pantry after their arguments many times. Sitting in her beach chair, she'd talk about how life is like swimming in the Mississippi River, full of whirlpools and tides you can't fight. In fact, if you fight them, it only gets worse. Many times, she'd sit back, exhausted, and tell me to try to stay thin and make money.

The renovation took a year, and Dad joked about how he and Mom would eat dinner while driving around in Bermuda since the windows of the house were all knocked out, or because the walls weren't insulated yet. When it was over, the kitchen was unrecognizable—nothing of the old one remained. All of the burners on the stove worked without throwing matches into them. The oven was run by a computer rather than by kicking it. The terra-cotta floor belonged in *House & Garden* magazine.

Amazingly, their relationship changed almost as dramatically. After years of living in separate bedrooms, of locking each other out and packing and unpacking suitcases, my father moved back into my mother's bedroom. I think they were even embarrassed about it. When I'd call home, they would be right there together, laughing over some joke one of them had just made. Instead of two people tired and bitter from fighting too much, they became like long-distance runners on an endorphin high. They were in love again.

The real proof of that came when my last surviving great-aunt, Mary, died. For a long time, she had been somewhat senile, inviting us for dinner and serving only English muffins. She would serve one round, then say, "How about an English muffin?" Then we'd start over again. We'd keep eating English muffins and strawberry jam until we couldn't stand it anymore.

After her death, my mother received a final inheritance, which she and my father could have lived on for the rest of their lives, if they were careful. But they have never been interested in being careful. My mother took the money and without threats or stipulations—without a memory, it seemed—she handed all of it over to my father to invest. She knew he would lose most of it, but I think for my parents, life wouldn't be interesting if disaster wasn't distinctly possible. For that reason, they always leave the car keys in the ignition, and the front doors of the house unlocked.

As with many love stories, money had a lot to do with my parents' tale—their love went up and down with their fortunes. It's interesting to see the paths my siblings and I have taken in our own love-and-money lives. My sister married a banker who makes tons of money. My brother, not yet married, is also a banker and makes even more. I, on the other hand, became a writer with paychecks that arrived about as regularly as shooting stars. Then, I married a dreamer who thinks about money about as often as he thinks about the oxygen system on a lunar spacecraft— never.

From my perspective, my sister and brother seem to glide through life. They fly first-class; their houses are air-conditioned and painfully neat. My husband and I, on the other hand, live more like my parents did. Our refrigerator leaks sizable puddles on the kitchen floor, invariably when dinner guests are over. Nothing about our lives is smooth. The zippers on most of our clothes stick. Even our driveway has potholes in it.

I actually appreciate those things the way my father appreciates sad country songs. From my parents, I learned that love is one part passion and nine parts hanging on for dear life, that hardship can safekeep love and maybe even give it more spark in the end. The feeling of roaring down a mountain on a toboggan and holding on for dear life is what love in my new, small family is about.

My parents now have their own stash of private, inside jokes—these days, many of them are about death. Nothing has ever scared them, death included. They talk about it all the time, the way teenagers discuss the prom. They also take drives together again. While my father used to go on his private disappearances, they now disappear together. For days, the phone will ring unanswered in their house, and just when I'm on the verge of calling the police or asking the neighbors to break in, my mother and father resurface, back from a drive to Cape Cod or the Jersey shore to swim in the ocean.

While both Mom and Dad are in incredible physical shape, both thin and athletic, I think of them as whales, nicked and scarred yet the strongest creatures in the ocean. How did they survive, wash up on the shore together, when they must have asked each other for a divorce five hundred times? I think in part because they allowed each other to go crazy when necessary. When times were the roughest with them, he let her garden all night. She let him smoke cigars and listen to Johnny Cash records over and over again. Both of them knew: it was an emergency.

I used to admire couples who seemed to glide through life, so in love it was as if they had casters on their shoes. I now admire the scrappers and the stumblers, the dreamers and the all-night gardeners. Maybe I even admire them more. I think that when your love life has real difficulty in it, it is easier to believe in heaven. Not because you think you'll get there someday, but because you miss it so much.

Every time my parents drove through Vermont during their on-the-verge-of-a-divorce years, they would make a detour and slowly pass by Cloudland, my mother's old family farm. If we were in the backseat, we'd say out loud what they were thinking silently—that's where we might have lived, high up near the clouds and surrounded by acres, if only our story had been a little different.

Now, I think even my parents would say they've found their way back to Cloudland.

Muddy

Waters

FOR SOME PEOPLE, falling in love is like an explosion—a sudden, unexpected, before-and-after kind of experience. For Ellen Butler and Eddy Bikales, it wasn't that way at all. Their relationship moved at the imperceptibly slow pace of an iceberg. It bore no resemblance to fireworks, lightning bolts, or other forms of combustion. It was more like a slow-burning beeswax candle. As Eddy says, "It took us over ten years to fall madly in love."

They met in the mid-eighties in Burlington, Vermont, a town Eddy describes as "a magnet for drifting twentysomethings." Ellen and Eddy both drifted there after college for the cheap rents, nonjudgmental people, high mountains, and frequent snowstorms. They were serious skiers who wanted to escape a nine-to-five life. But otherwise, they were nothing alike.

Eddy was handsome, tan, rugged, and raggedy. Gregarious and energetic to the point of skittish, his conversations rarely lasted longer than a chairlift ride. He lived with a roommate named Punky and a mutt named Yo Bud! in an apartment with a hole the size of a hubcap in the living room wall. He often threw big parties where he'd hold out a hat for donations, which he would use to order pizzas for everybody. "When I met Ellen I was still living like a college student," he said. "I stayed in the mode of keg parties long after the bell had tolled."

One of his favorite hangouts in Burlington was Muddy Waters, a café where customers could find everything on the bulletin board from a lesbian lover to a used pair of skis to a live-in baby-sitting job. Inside, Muddy Waters had the atmosphere of a hollowed-out tree, with mahogany walls and gnarly tables made out of branches and logs, some with the bark still on them. The people who hung out in Muddy Waters never appeared to be affected by caffeine. They behaved instead as if they were drinking chamomile tea, reading for hours, mellow as wind chimes, easygoing as willow trees. Eddy fit right in.

He was in his mid-twenties, and although he had a master's degree in environmental studies, he had decided not to use it. "I've never really known what to do with my life," he said. "After I got my master's degree, all the people who graduated with me went off and got jobs, and I just couldn't bear the thought of it. I couldn't stomach it. So I got a job in a sub shop. I just didn't want to be one of the great masses of men who went off to live lives of quiet desperation. Plus, I didn't want any money. I was perfectly happy living under the poverty line. I would go to all-you-can-eat buffets and eat chicken wings with blue cheese dressing and celery sticks. I was the master of food deals. I'd go to the Hare Krishna place for free dinners. I'd always cut out coupons in the paper for free cereal. Most of my clothes were from the Salvation Army, and I would get one haircut a year. I'd get it cut really short, and then I'd let it grow until I looked like Jackson Browne."

When it came to possessions, he was almost militantly unmaterialistic. "I had a little Honda Accord hatchback, and my policy was, I could get everything I owned into my Honda Accord," he said. "Whenever I bought something new, I'd throw out something else the same size. If I bought a pair of sneakers, for instance, I'd throw out a dictionary."

Ellen could not have been more different. Refined rather than raggedy, she lived in a pretty, old wooden house with stained-glass windows, honey-colored polished floors, and bookcases full of classic novels. While Eddy was wild and could be counted on to wear a lampshade on his head at parties, she was shy and introverted. It was her nature to sit as still as a cat. She liked long, soul-searching heart-to-heart talks. She was polite and proper, and sometimes regretted it—she once wrote an essay for a Burlington paper about NOT losing her virginity in high school and how that had made her feel like a complete failure. She was endearingly earnest—even her pageboy haircut had a blunt honesty to it—and her spirit was as natural and clear as a Vermont stream. Eddy was the rough ocean.

"In college, I was very concerned about my work and grades, and Eddy was the type of person who yelled outside my window bothering me at night," Ellen said. "I cared about rules and propriety and not bothering other people, and he ran in the opposite direction."

While they instantly recognized each other as opposites rather than soul mates when they met, Eddy and Ellen did share one main attribute—a sense of being lost. They saw the world very similarly. For them, their friends seemed to divide into two groups after college—people who were busy and looked at their watches constantly and people who never knew exactly what time it was. Eddy and Ellen both belonged to the second group. They spent their time dreaming about the day when they would figure out how to make their mark on the world, which often seemed as impossible as making a mark on a shooting star. But they were both optimistic people. They had small wardrobes and enormous hopes.

To get by, Eddy taught skiing in the winter, ran inn-to-inn bike tours in the summer, worked as a bartender, and once even started a boat waxing business. "I discovered that I basically don't like to work," he said. "My parents had tried to tell me my whole life that the main joys of living come from work. They told me that over and over again, but that's just not the case for me. I'm happiest when I'm working the least. So I started this company called Biff's Boat Shine. I would clean boats and wax them. The idea was I'd only have to work half the year."

Ellen also changed jobs and life plans often—she wrote

autobiographical essays for a local paper, halfheartedly
filled out medical school applications, briefly worked as a
dance critic, waitressed on and off, and even dabbled with
unemployment temporarily. "For a while, I joined the great
wandering jobless in Burlington," she said. "Burlington is a
great place to be when you're twenty-one and have no idea
what to do with your life. Everyone is really outdoorsy and
friendly and no one judges you. There was a whole group
of women who got together on Monday nights to have a
potluck. When I think of Burlington, I think of potlucks."

After they met, Ellen and Eddy drifted into a relationship
the same way they drifted into jobs—partly by accident,
partly as an experiment, and partly out of high hopes. At
first, they hung out together mainly because everyone else
they knew was busy during the day. "One of our main at-
tractions to each other was we both wandered through life a
little aimlessly in our twenties," Eddy said. "That's definitely
one of the things we had in common. Our friends were going off and having Lands' End lives—husbands and jobs and
careers—and we were the flounderers in Burlington."

Their first kiss happened in an almost desultory way,
with just enough spark there to kiss again. After that, their
romance flickered on and off like a lamp with bad wiring. It
was five years before they called each other girlfriend and
boyfriend. Even then they rarely got together more than
once a week, and sometimes their connection was so fragile it seemed as if they were trying to peel an orange in one
long, continuous strip. At any moment, the connection
could break for good. For a long time, they told friends

they were "in like" with each other. Still, they stuck it out with one another. When asked what he thought kept them together in the absence of infatuation, strong attraction, chemistry, or even great kisses, Eddy said, "Inertia." When they slept in the same bed, he always turned his back to her.

In their early years together, their relationship was the warmest when they were outside together in the cold. Eddy took Ellen on one adventure after another, and she eventually became his main partner for mountain climbing, skiing, skating, tobogganing, and bar-hopping. "I'd moved to Burlington ready for any adventure—the crazier the idea, the better the adventure," Eddy said. "I just totally believe you have to live every day as if it's your last. That's one of the reasons I could never hold a real job. Why work every day if you're going to die next week?"

One time, he knocked on the door of Ellen's house at midnight, asking if she wanted to climb a mountain. A full moon was out, and he had a great idea: he wanted to see if they could make it to the top of the mountain without flashlights. They did, feeling their way up the trails in total darkness with their arms stretched out like sleepwalkers. To add to the challenge, Eddy made another rule as they started their climb: they had to talk in French until they reached the top (they made it). Another time, Eddy and Ellen drove all the way to Canada one night, on desolate back roads, as curvy as creeks, and rockier. Eddy drove with the headlights off most of the way.

Whenever she was with Eddy, Ellen was usually terrified, but she always forced herself to go on his adventures, like someone forcing herself to drink tequila with a scorpion at the bottom of the glass. "I was very straight at the time, and here was this guy full of mischief," she said. "He was a bad boy, he looked very antiestablishment in a lot of ways. He tipped cows over, he wore red lipstick to parties, he had lots and lots of friends. His carefree way of life was totally mysterious to me. I was living a very serious life. I saw him as my access to fun so I made this commitment that I would go on any adventure with him."

Almost every winter, they skied across Lake Champlain together as soon as the water froze. "One of the things that made me fall much more in like with Ellen is that when Lake Champlain froze over, we were always the first ones to ski across," Eddy remembers. "It was often very treacherous. We were never totally sure it was frozen. But she always came across with me. Here was Ellen, who doesn't look like the most adventurous type, who seems cultured and sophisticated and reserved, but she was up for anything. I kept expecting her to say no, but she never did."

Whenever they went skiing on the lake, they stopped to listen to the water underneath. They would lie down next to each other, sprawled out in their parkas like collapsed snowmen, with their ears close to the ice as if they were eavesdropping on a conversation in another room. "Being out on the ice is like being in the desert," Ellen said. "It's all white and it's freezing cold and it's this weird terrain that moves under you and makes all these popping and creaking noises. It's like listening to whales."

In many ways, their relationship was like the surface of Lake Champlain at the beginning of winter. They were never sure if it was solid or not. It would seem sturdy as rock one moment, then fragile as old lace the next. But they kept on, one step at a time, ready to fall through at any moment and often surprised when the ground actually held.

"We did not have a whirlwind romance," Ellen said. "I never got swept off my feet by Eddy, which I'm kind of bummed about. I never had that 'He's the one!' feeling. We just basically hung out until we got to know each other well enough to see how compatible we are."

Gradually, as they spent more time together, Ellen became more adventuresome, funnier, a little louder, and much more limber. Eddy affected her like a yoga class, slowly loosening and extending her. One night, soon after they declared themselves boyfriend and girlfriend, she remembers driving down a winding, dirt country road by herself and impulsively turning off the headlights just as Eddy would. For miles, she navigated by the light of the stars and the moon. If love can be measured by the changes it brings, that was the night she began to realize she was falling out of 'like' and into love.

It took Eddy a lot longer to use the words *Ellen* and *love* in the same sentence, even the same conversation. Like a child making marks on the wall to show how much he had grown since his last birthday, Eddy measured his affection for her in small increments. Each year, he felt a little more in like with her. One winter, about six years after they met, Eddy remembers they were skiing across Lake Champlain when his ski pole broke, miles from shore. They didn't have any food with them; the ice cracked like an old wooden chair about to collapse; snow was swirling around and blowing in their eyes like shards of glass; and as they slowly made their way back, Eddy worried they might be walking in circles.

"Most people would have totally panicked in that situation, but Ellen was levelheaded and funny," he said. "Her sense of humor was amazing. She kept me laughing all the way back across. After that, I liked her more. But I wasn't in love or enamored yet. Enamored would be overstating it."

Whenever they were out on the ice or just hanging out, they never, ever talked about their relationship. They talked about politics, Madonna, the wilderness, Paris, ski wax, religion, but not about themselves. "We had a custom of not talking about our relationship, which kept us together, I think," Ellen said. "I'd had so many overintellectualized relationships where we'd talked everything out—why you do this, how I feel about that. When you have to do that nuts-and-bolts talking, you're past the point of no return, I believe. The love is over. It's such a huge pitfall in coupledom, when people talk and try to change each other. I don't have any faith in talk."

Just as there are all kinds of textures and moods of snow, from light and feathery to heavy and sticky, Eddy went through just as many different feelings about Ellen, but one feeling he absolutely never had about her was certainty. "I was dubious of our relationship because I wasn't knocked off my feet by Ellen," Eddy said. "I was not madly in love. I always thought I would meet my soul mate and, boom, I'd know right away. I did once meet a woman that way, in Montana, in an airport bar. We hit it off so well, within twenty minutes I felt like I'd known her forever. She even believed we'd met in a past life, that we had been together in Denmark hundreds of years ago. It was crazy, but on some level I believed it, too. For years, I looked for that instant connection, and if I didn't feel it right away, I gave up. With Ellen, because she didn't knock my socks off at first, I thought, She's not my soul mate. Everything was fun and groovy, but I didn't think she was *the one*."

After years of adventures on the ice and sleeping back to back, Eddy and Ellen eventually began to sense their relationship was ending, the way you can sense a snowfall ending, even when it's still snowing. Eddy had begun to watch other women more closely, to be mesmerized by their pale blue eyes or slim silver thumb rings, the little details that pull a person away. And Ellen had begun to notice a handsome novelist in town who had a great way with sentences. For months, both Eddy and Ellen thought about the letter they should write to the other, saying it was over and why. They imagined the message they might leave on the other's answering machine, or the song they would play that said it all.

Eddy remembers, "When I finally called to break up, Ellen said, 'Oh, that's such a relief. I was about to call you to do the same thing.' I was really psyched. I thought it was going to be such a terrible phone call, and instead it was great. We broke up, and then said good-bye on a very high note."

The next morning, Eddy's phone rang. It was Ellen. Like her haircut, she was perfectly blunt. "I'm not done with you," she said.

She asked for a "summit," a weekend away together. "I said I had already made weekend plans," remembers Eddy. "And she said, 'Break 'em.' That amazed me. It was so bold and gutsy. So I met her for the weekend."

They spent three days together in Pennsylvania, in a log cabin in the woods. "On the way, I said to myself, 'I'm going to be totally honest with her,'" recalls Eddy. "'It may be hard for her to take the honest bitter truth, which was, Look, I don't love you.'"

He never got around to saying that. They spent the weekend on the couch discussing their relationship as methodically as someone counting and comparing snowflakes. "We talked and talked and talked," said Eddy. "And I just felt myself falling and falling, and I looked at her one minute and I was in love with her! It happened right there on the couch. I knew the moment it hit me, *boom*. That weekend, we broke up and fell in love. I said, 'I love you; now what are we going to do?'"

They did not get back together. Instead, they came up with an idea as challenging as walking to the top of a mountain speaking French the whole way: They made a pact not to speak to each other for a year. They would date other people, purposefully forget each other, put all pictures of each other away in a drawer, and see what happened. Then, they would meet in exactly one year, to compare notes and to see if they still had feelings for each other or if they were as numb around each other as people who have been out skiing all day.

Ellen spent the year in a serious relationship with the novelist. She later called him the Anti-Eddy. "He was the guy who talked about his feelings too much and he cried all the time," she said.

She even moved in with him for a while, but his habits soon irritated Ellen—he slept late, disliked dinner parties, and would rather be shot in the head than climb a mountain while speaking French or ski out on the ice at the beginning of winter. "He only made me miss Eddy more," she said.

Meanwhile, Eddy dated several women—a lawyer, a model, a skier, a waitress, and a poet. "I dated many wonderful women that year, really great women," he said. "They were beautiful, interesting people, but it always felt forced. The more I dated, the more I thought, 'They're not Ellen.' I missed talking to Ellen, I missed our adventures. It was so easy with her."

After a year of not speaking, Ellen and Eddy met in a café on the appointed day. He arrived first and watched the door the way someone might watch the surface of a lake after his best friend had dived in and stayed under a little too long. He was terrified she wouldn't appear or, worse, that she'd fallen in love with someone else. Ellen finally walked in, with her same practical pageboy haircut and no makeup, not a stunning beauty but definitely the woman he wanted to marry. He was finally madly in love with her.

During their year apart, they had both found interesting careers that they had stuck with—he had begun working as a documentary filmmaker and she as a correspondent for "The World," a show on National Public Radio. They were in their thirties now. No longer flounderers or drifters, they worked long hours, wore watches, and carried around laptop computers as naturally as they used to carry skis.

Within months, Eddy and Ellen moved in together, and they easily combined his burritos-and-plastic-forks spirit with her preference for real silver and pot roasts. "From the start, living together was a breeze," Eddy says. "We didn't have any squabbles, we didn't fight over blankets or piles of clutter. We didn't use the M-word. We were both working about a hundred hours a week so we would meet for brushing our teeth and maybe read a poem before we went to bed. That was our relationship."

After about a year of living together, a completely unexpected thing happened: Eddy began to hear *his* biological clock ticking very loudly. "It never crossed my mind that I would ever marry or have children," he said. "I was a big environmentalist, and I thought kids were a burden on the world. Also, I just believed life was too much fun. I couldn't imagine what joy there could be in following around a toddler in your apartment when you could be out winter camping. But I suddenly really wanted children."

During the winter of 1995, in the middle of a blizzard, he asked Ellen to marry him. "It was a magical time, " he said. "No stores or offices were open. People were skiing in the streets. We had *days* together. One afternoon, we took a bottle of wine, chairs, and a table and put them out in the middle of our road and took a photo of ourselves. It was freezing and I just said, 'So, Ellen, when are we going to have kids?'"

They were married in May 1997, in Burlington, on the stage of the movie theater downtown where the marquee read: "Eddy and Ellen Get Hitched." They had finally become a passionate, inseparable, madly-in-love couple, two people who look into each other's eyes as if they are totally amazed at their luck in finding each other. When together, they seem to move as if an invisible string were tied between them, each reacting to the other's slightest gesture like partners in a two-legged race. Their wedding invitation read: "It took us a while to realize that all the hanging out we've been doing together was making us into a couple. But it has and come Memorial Day weekend, we would love to see you at our wedding."

Looking back on their long relationship now, Eddy says it was like grapevines, uncertain and vulnerable to the slightest change in weather or atmosphere for a long, long time. But it never stopped growing. "It just kept getting better and better, all the way through to the present," he said. "It's been a very slow train to We."

Ellen compares them to a nineteenth-century couple married off by their parents, two young people who needed many years to figure out how to fall in love with each other. "When my friends ask for love advice, I tell them, 'If the relationship isn't so great at first, maybe it will grow into something,'" Ellen says. "I know a lot of people who go out and meet someone and decide yes or no right away. People trust their instincts much more than they should. At first, I had tons of complaints about Eddy. I don't now, but I did for years."

Recalling their early, lackluster kisses and the way they used to sleep back to back, Ellen added, "I also think sexual attraction is way overplayed. People probably destroy a lot of good things in the absence of that."

When you meet them now, it is hard to believe Eddy and Ellen were once so blasé about each other, or that they were such different characters when they met. Eddy, who lived for years in a hovel with a hole in the wall, is now in charge of redecorating their new, sprawling, grown-up home in a doorman apartment building in New York City. On a recent visit, he was in the middle of a meeting with an interior decorator, discussing fabrics and period furniture. Ellen, on the other hand, is still serene but no longer quiet. She says she is so much wilder now, much more collegiate than she used to be even as a college student. She laughs easily, interrupts Eddy when she wants to, runs for the telephone when it rings, drinks beer from the bottle. When she looks back on her early days with Eddy, she quotes her favorite Joni Mitchell song: "'I was so much older then. I'm younger than that now.'"

Love Is

Blind

REAL LOVE, I've learned, is a very, very strong form of forgiveness, and I think that's partly why so many people yearn for it so much. I don't think people yearn for love because they hate staying home alone on Saturday night or because they dread going into restaurants alone and saying "Just one" to the maître d' for the millionth time. People want love because they want their taped-together eyeglasses, unstylish clothes, or lack of athletic ability to be forgiven. They want someone to look right past the surface stuff like bad hair days, a laugh that's too loud, strange family members, or potato chips crunching underneath the couch pillows whenever anyone sits down.

When William Neumann met Richelle Sasz, he was blind to many things about her that others found glaring. He first saw her in a crowded nightclub in Cancún, Mexico.

She was with a few girlfriends, and although she was leaning on a pair of crutches and wearing braces on her legs, those weren't the first things he noticed about her. "Just looking at her, I could see she was so upbeat," he said. "She had a perky look, she was very spunky and very aggressive. She wasn't somebody who felt sorry for herself. Nothing was going to stop her. She was out on the dance floor! You don't see many disabled people at clubs. But she doesn't think she's disabled."

Richelle grew up near the ocean on Long Island, in an all-American, middle-class neighborhood with block after block of ranch houses and capes, many with hot rods, souped-up pickups, and boats parked in the driveway. Until she became disabled in high school, Richelle was a cheerleader—she could do perfect splits even in a pair of tight blue jeans. At home, she and her three older sisters shared one bathroom, which made her even more patient and easygoing than she was naturally. Her oldest sister, Debbie, owned the most clothes and was known for locking them in a closet protected with multiple padlocks. But whenever Debbie left the house, Richelle and her other sisters would pry open the door by unscrewing the padlocks or, if that didn't work, they'd take the entire door off its hinges and steal all the clothes.

In high school, Richelle was popular—one year, she was voted Class Flirt, Best Personality, and Most Spirited. Besides being a quintessential, blond, athletic cheerleader, she was also known for break-dancing in the school hallways. "She was on a break-dancing team," said Denise

MacNamara-Bandl, her best friend from high school. "Oh my God, she used to do headspins that would last forever."

She also drove to school, which added to her popularity, even though her car was a brown, beat-up Camaro that stalled all the time. "It was a hand-me-down from her sisters," said Denise. "It was probably the ugliest car I ever saw."

One October morning in 1986, the Camaro didn't start, so Richelle caught a ride with Denise and another friend, Tommy. Richelle describes her state of mind that morning this way: "I had just started eleventh grade and I was dating one of the most popular guys in school," she said. "I couldn't believe I got him."

On the way to school, the three friends got into a freak car accident, catching the bumper of another car and fish-tailing out of control. Richelle was thrown out the back window and flew ten feet through the air and into a tree. "At first they couldn't find me," she remembers. "They were screaming, 'Where is Richelle? Where is Richelle?' I was going in and out of consciousness. The next thing I remember is being in the ambulance and they were cutting up my sister's winter jacket and I was thinking, Oh my God, my sister is going to kill me. They're cutting up her new jacket."

As it turned out, Richelle had injured her spine during the accident and was paralyzed from the waist down. The doctors said she had zero chance of walking again. Instead of going back to high school, she stayed in the hospital for months, then went to wheelchair school. There are certain things you never want to experience—such as what it feels like to drown or to be homeless—and living in a wheelchair is one of them. "I learned how to cook in a wheelchair, how to set the table, how to get dishes out of cabinets, brush my hair, work a blow-dryer," Richelle remembers. "I don't know if you'd call it denial or positive thinking, but I kept saying, 'Why are you teaching me this stuff? I'm not going to be in a wheelchair.'"

A year after the accident, she returned to high school, driving a car outfitted with special hand controls, with her wheelchair folded up in the backseat like an enormous winged insect. "I went from being one of the popular girls in school to being in a wheelchair," she said. "The people around me were very scared. Guys definitely looked at me differently. No one, *no one* wanted to date me. They wanted to be friends, but they couldn't see past the disability. It was definitely too strange. They wondered, 'Do I open doors for her or let her do it herself? What if she falls, what do I do?' It's just a big question mark. I made up for it by proving myself—I wanted to prove I could still have a lot of fun."

She did. Friends say she never let the wheelchair slow her down. She soon resumed her car pool, picking up the same friends she drove to school before the accident. On Saturday nights, she went out dancing with friends—she would wheel out into the middle of the dance floor and shimmy from the waist up without any self-consciousness at all. She went everywhere a wheelchair could go, and whenever her wheelchair got stuck—on bumpy sidewalks or at the bottom of the bleachers at basketball games—she would just get out and crawl. Or she would ask friends for piggyback rides.

"We used to bring her *everywhere*," said Denise. "I would bring her to the beach and walk with her on my back. I'd always take her to parties, and even though she was sitting there in a wheelchair, she never let it bother her. She was funny, too, because she wouldn't hesitate to ask a guy she didn't know, 'Would you mind picking me up and carrying me over there?' Guys loved it."

Sometimes Richelle's sisters carried her places, taking hold of her legs and arms and transporting her like a huge starfish: "I remember once my sister and her friend took me to Friendly's," Richelle said. "They carried me out of the car—my sister took one arm and one leg and her friend took the other arm and leg. We were laughing so hard. My friends would pick me up all the time and carry me around all over the place."

After high school, Richelle spent two years in intense physical therapy, learning to walk again. At first, she began walking with clunky, thigh-high metal braces, which made her lurch like the Tin Man in *The Wizard of Oz*. Then, after her legs strengthened, she started walking with high-top Reebok sneakers and white plastic calf-high braces that look like lightweight ski boots. "Walking is such a wonderful thing," she said. "It's an awesome feeling. You're upright, you're getting exercise, you're seeing eye-to-eye with people, you're able to dance on your feet, you're able to reach things in the cabinet, you're able to walk down stairs instead of crawling down them. You're talking about two different worlds, a wheelchair and walking."

Even once she started walking again, Richelle's love life ranged from nonexistent to tragicomic. "I clearly remember once when I was dating a guy and I was at his house and I had to go down these stairs that didn't have any kind of railing," she said. "I actually fell down the stairs and into a bush. When I fall, I usually laugh and people who know me laugh, but strangers freak out completely. Everyone screams, 'Oh my God! Oh my God!' People just freak out when a disabled person falls. I always feel bad for the person who's picking me up."

If guys ever approached her at parties or in nightclubs, it was usually to ask what was wrong with her. "A lot of guys thought, She's really pretty but she's disabled," Richelle said. "I had one guy come up to me in a bar and say, 'Oh my God, can you have sex?' Since I wear braces on my legs and walk with crutches, they think nothing else works properly."

When she was twenty-two, Richelle moved into New York City by herself, enrolled in college, and got a part-time job at Just One Break, an employment agency for disabled people. In New York, she continued going out to parties and nightclubs with friends, and she became even more daring on the dance floor, occasionally climbing up on top of the bar and dancing, usually while holding on tight to the hands of a girlfriend. If people stared, she ignored them. Although Richelle sometimes loses her balance—she has fallen on crowded sidewalks, tripped while walking out of elevators, tumbled onto the carpet before a roomful of men in business suits—her personality is incredibly grounded and even-keeled. "It's hard to stay positive, but it's harder to be depressed and negative," she said, summing up her overall philosophy. "You can either choose to be upset or you can choose to get over it, move on."

While some people in wheelchairs or on crutches look slumped and sad, Richelle is the opposite. She's as cheerful as someone in a Breck shampoo commercial. She still looks like a cheerleader, with her waist-length blond hair, freckles, perfect teeth, and sparkly blue eyes. Naturally gregarious and very funny, she befriends strangers everywhere—in elevators, bars, workout gyms, grocery stores, airports. She wears bikinis and miniskirts, letting her braces show rather than trying to hide them.

When William saw her in a bikini, he thought she looked beautiful. The son of a fireman, William grew up with three older sisters in Watchung, New Jersey, in an eighteenth-century house with very low ceilings, enormous fireplaces, and walls insulated with horsehair and mud. He skis, scuba dives, drives a green pickup truck, works as a construction supervisor, and looks like Tom Cruise with curly hair and wire-rimmed glasses. While he has the muscular build of a rugby player, he also has the soft-spoken, patient, sweet temperament of a poet. "As a child, I was surrounded by females," he said. "I think it made me more sensitive. My sisters taught me to have patience, to bake. They even had me crocheting."

His sisters recall he was a cross between Dennis the Menace and a monk, both mischievous and deeply sensitive. "He used to booby-trap the kitchen," said one sister, Lori Iverson. "He would take fishing line and put pots on it so when I came home late from a date, I'd make noise coming through. He also put hermit crabs and rubber worms in my bed."

On the other hand, when one of his grandmothers entered a nursing home after a stroke, William was the one who visited her most often, lying beside her in bed and telling stories. At the time he was seventeen, an age when most people think of nursing homes as haunted houses.

In Cancún, Richelle and William ended up spending a week together by the pool, sharing drinks the color of tropical sunsets and talking about everything except why she wore braces on her legs. "It was like he never saw my crutches or braces," Richelle said. "For him, other qualities of mine outshone the crutches. He saw me for who I was and he didn't see the disability."

Finally, she said to him one afternoon by the pool, "So, do you want to know what happened to me?"

Unlike most other men Richelle met, William was more interested in her great jokes and sparkly presence than her accident. "I knew something had happened," he said. "I saw her in the pool and I saw her scars, but I was interested in *her*. When you find the right person, you see past certain things and concentrate on the positive side. I just didn't think about her disability that much."

OVER THE YEARS of writing about love, I have met so many people who never thought they'd find someone who'd overlook their imperfections, sad experiences, meager bank accounts, or complicated lives.

One of my most inspiring interviews was with Wendy Williams, an overweight woman who figured she had about as much chance of falling in love as she did of finding a dress her size in the boutiques on Rodeo Drive in Hollywood. Men were rarely nice, let alone flirtatious, around Wendy. Growing up in a small New England town, she recalls guys screaming as she passed by, "Look at her! She'd crush you."

Until she was in her late thirties, Wendy felt happy, even proud, to be single. She lived in Newton, Massachusetts, in an apartment filled with scented candles; she loved her job as a nurse; she was active in the local Presbyterian church; she listened to public radio and alternative rock stations; and she never obsessed about men, love, or becoming a bride. "I was brought up in the throes of feminism, and I was quite content not to be man hungry," she says. "My attitude was, Let an enlightened smart man come find me."

Her attitude changed almost overnight when she was thirty-seven and two of her best friends were diagnosed with breast cancer. She suddenly realized there was a possibility she could die before an enlightened smart man found her. So she decided to begin her own search for a husband. "I rolled up my sleeves and told myself, Just go for it," she recalls. "The first thing I did was place a personal ad in *Boston* magazine. I thought, 'There's a needle-in-the-haystack principle here. I'm going to go through person after person until I find someone I like."

She also answered personal ads, reading them with a big Magic Marker in hand, circling, starring, and crossing off people while sitting in her apartment late at night.

"I was looking for tongue-in-cheek humor and a droll, fun attitude that showed the person writing the ad got the fact that this is a lark," she says. "If I read an ad like, 'I'm a forty-year-old gentleman who loves long walks and wine before the fireplace,' I'd gag and cross that off. If they said anything about their earning capacity, I just walked right past them. That's not what I consider important. It spoke volumes when people spelled out, 'I want a five-foot two-inch blonde with blue eyes who works out ten times a week.' It seemed like they were trying to replace something they'd lost."

Wendy, who is blond, five-nine, and weighs 250 pounds, finally met Jeff, her future husband, through a voice-mail personal ad. She was the one who placed the ad; he responded with a recorded message. When she heard it, Wendy immediately liked him.

"He sounded very quiet and subdued," she remembers. "He said, 'I have two boys and they are the most important things in my life and I positively do not, I repeat do not, like any sports. I really like bluegrass music and I've just recently taken a class on *King Lear* and I keep mulling over King Lear's life."

Wendy called Jeff and they hit it off so instantly, it was almost eerie. One of the first things he told her was, "Wendy, don't worry about your weight. I wear glasses and have a beard and I'm not the tallest guy in the world."

For Wendy, meeting Jeff was better than finding a miracle diet pill—he didn't even care about her weight problem.

Jean McFadden, another bride I interviewed, never thought a man would be able to see past her complicated, sad life story. A young widow, she was supporting herself as a cook when I met her, preparing meals for homebound people with AIDS. At a party one night, she was introduced to Edward Layton, a student of acupuncture and Chinese herbal medicine. "I tended to really scare men off," Jean said. "I was in med school, which terrifies a lot of men, and I was married before and my prior husband died, and I worked for an AIDS organization. Most of the men went screaming into the night, but Ed looked at all that and said, 'Cool.'"

SIMILARLY, after William got to know Richelle—crutches, scars, and all—he said, "Cool." William has been her steady boyfriend ever since they met in Cancún. Now twenty-eight and twenty-nine, they share a high-rise apartment in New York City, a place so uncluttered and neat even the wastebaskets are empty and spotless. Sometimes, if you look closely at the white walls, you can see fingerprint marks, like pale shell prints on a beach. Richelle often uses the wall for support when she's walking around the apartment, and every few months William repaints the entire place. Richelle still walks in high-top sneakers and lightweight braces, and her closet is full of identical black Reeboks, like shoes lined up in a bowling alley.

When William introduced Richelle to his parents, they were almost as blind to her disability as he had been. "When I first saw her, she drove in my driveway in a white convertible Infiniti and I thought she was a movie star," remembered William's father. "She was very pretty and self-confident."

While covering weddings, the couples I love the most are ones like Richelle and William, Wendy and Jeff, and Jean and Ed, the ones who don't see each other's weaknesses or problems, who forgive all kinds of quirky habits, baggage, and history. I covered a wedding recently where the bride read a passage from a poem, thanking her new husband for ignoring so many unlikable things about her—including her habit of wearing a big black mask to bed every night to help her sleep.

Meeting Richelle and William also taught me the importance of politeness between lovers. They are kind, easygoing people, especially with each other. A wedding guest once told me she thought the thing that made love last was not chemistry, humor, or dancing in the kitchen to slow Patsy Cline songs, although those things help. The real thing that preserves love, she said, is good manners—being courteous and considerate, not slamming doors or throwing insults around like a football, thinking about the other person the way a perfect host might think about a guest— what will make you happy?

Richelle and William have amazing manners with each other. For his sake, she rarely complains. When the weather is bad and her legs hurt, she stays quiet and still like a bird waiting out a rainstorm. For her sake, he thinks of ways to make the usually cumbersome and mechanical act of dressing up more fun for her—for a party they went to recently, he spray-painted her Reeboks and crutches to match her clothes. Soon after they started dating, he taught her how to scuba dive, since that's the one sport where it's impossible to fall down. "Once we're in the water, she's totally independent," William said. "She's a fish. Nothing holds her back like on land. Sometimes I try to picture her in real life on land without crutches and braces. I've seen videotapes of her before the accident. I watched a couple of tapes of her in beauty pageants, and it was really interesting seeing her in high heels. I knew it was something I'd never see in real life. I love shoes, probably because I have three sisters, and Richelle is limited to sneakers."

When I was in my early twenties and thinking about love nearly constantly, I had a very clear idea of what it would be like to finally find THE ONE. I imagined falling in love would be like putting sunglasses on—first of all, I'd suddenly feel thinner. Also, the look of my entire world would change. Once I fell in love I'd no longer live in my tiny basement studio apartment, where all the doorknobs wobbled like loose teeth and I was eye level with the sidewalk and could watch people walking by all day in their old, beat-up shoes.

I no longer think of love that way, partly because once I found love I continued living in places with bad views and wobbly doorknobs. But mostly, from meeting couples like Richelle and William, I've learned that love changes your mood more than anything else. Falling in love is not about upgrading your apartment car or dining room furniture; it's about improving your emotional state. Richelle and William live in a small, simple apartment with only a few pieces of furniture, a tiny kitchen table, a flowery couch, a television. It is not the sort of place Ralph Lauren would ever use for a photo shoot. But in their little unglamorous home, they've created a reprieve, a place where Richelle is not disabled. Together, they filter out the negative, the insulting, the depressing. Richelle and William are as determined to find the bright side of things as little kids are to find hidden Easter eggs.

"People think if you're in a wheelchair or you're on crutches, you have a bad life," Richelle said. "You can't possibly be happy. But I'm a really happy person. I just don't let anything get me down." The greatest favor people in love can do for each other, I learned from Richelle and William, is to at least *pretend* that life is easy.

Nowadays, William sometimes carries Richelle when she needs to be carried. On a recent trip to the Caribbean, he carried her every day from their beach chairs across the bumpy, hard-to-navigate sand and into the deep water, where she would take off like a dolphin. "When you truly love somebody so much, it doesn't matter what has happened to them," Richelle said. "You live with them and work it out no matter what comes up. That's what love is—it's understanding, it's helping, it's aiding the other person, it's encouraging them to be a better person, it's believing in them and giving them the strength to believe in themselves. It's lifting them up when they can't lift themselves up."

A Potluck

Romance

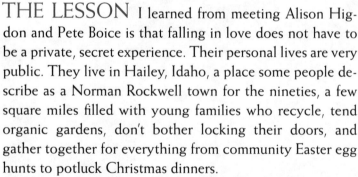

THE LESSON I learned from meeting Alison Higdon and Pete Boice is that falling in love does not have to be a private, secret experience. Their personal lives are very public. They live in Hailey, Idaho, a place some people describe as a Norman Rockwell town for the nineties, a few square miles filled with young families who recycle, tend organic gardens, don't bother locking their doors, and gather together for everything from community Easter egg hunts to potluck Christmas dinners.

The town is outside of Sun Valley, surrounded by mountains and filled with colorful wooden houses, many with wind chimes, cats, and skis on the porches. Alison, twenty-six, and Peter, thirty-four, live in an old green-and-eggplant-purple house set amidst vegetable, flower, berry, and herb gardens. There are also plum and apricot trees in their backyard, planted by Chinese miners a century ago, that now shade Pete's many kayaks.

Like most of their neighbors, Alison and Pete each moved to Hailey from other parts of the country. An outdoorsman and avid traveler—even his checks are decorated with skis and snow-covered peaks—Pete drove into town in 1988 in a Volkswagen Rabbit, planning to spend the winter skiing. "I had spent the summer in Alaska where I met a woman who wanted to buy a fishing boat, so we moved to Seattle," he said. "Then, when that didn't work out, I drove to Sun Valley."

In his family, Peter was nicknamed Mr. Free Spirit. He was known as the wanderer, the one destined to put the most miles on his cars. "From the time he was a little boy, Peter has always been a very sweet and dreamy child," said his aunt, Mrs. Mandeville Frost. "He was always eager to go out and see what else was out there. He started out in Alta, Utah, then went to Alaska, then went to Nepal. All the time, he made his family feel we were there with him. He would send pictures and tapes and wonderful writings, from everywhere. He has a ninety-two-year-old grandfather to whom he has sent wonderful descriptions of mountains and streams around the world."

Alison, a natural beauty who often wears flowers woven in her long red hair, arrived in Hailey by Greyhound bus in 1991. "I ended up in Hailey after working as an au pair in Germany," she said. "My sister lived here, so I packed up my bags and came out and moved into an old, dilapidated miner's shack. It had no insulation, a big huge woodstove, and a little ladder going upstairs into a loft area. There are so many wealthy people around here, I found a brand-new blue carpet at the dump."

Unlike many people in Hailey, Alison is not athletic—she likes to sew quilts, garden, and cook, and her favorite outdoor sport is sledding on cookie tins. "Alison is the only other person I know who's not embarrassed to be seen sledding in Hailey," said Laura Silber, a friend and fellow resident. "There are very extreme hard-core athletes out here. No one will do anything unless it's dangerous, exciting, and life-threatening."

Still, Alison felt comfortable in Hailey, found a job as a decorative painter, furnished her cabin with finds from the dump, and decided to stay. "I fell in love with how connected everyone was in the community," she said.

In Hailey, people are very, very connected. There's almost always a community event of some kind going on, whether it's digging out someone's truck from a snowbank, collecting flowers for a wedding, constructing a snowman, or helping out with a home birth. Each fall, the entire community gets together to pick fallen fruit from trees all over town, then meets in the park for a huge cider-pressing party. At Christmas, there's a big potluck dinner. On Easter day, eggs are hidden all over town, in backyards and gardens, and everyone is invited on the hunt. Each July, there's an open-invitation lip-synch-contest-and-Mexican-potluck-party. The community spirit in Hailey is so strong that when Laura, Alison's sister, got sick after giving birth, a group of women in town pitched in and breast-fed her baby until Laura recovered.

Alison first met Pete around the time of Hailey's cider-pressing party. "A friend and I went around the community and knocked on people's doors and asked them for apples and pears that had fallen on the ground," remembers Alison. "And Peter had a mini orchard in his backyard so we knocked on his door. I remember he had on a baseball cap and he was eating broccoli from the garden." To Alison, he seemed like the kind of guy who would go to a party in bare feet, buy his clothes in thrift shops, and pick wildflowers for his dinner table, which is just the sort of woman she is.

They met again, months later, at the community Easter egg hunt and party. Alison was one of the people hiding eggs in gardens and yards around town. "I thought Alison was incredibly beautiful and I just liked her aura," recalls Pete, who works as a house painter and kayaking instructor. "I can still remember what she was wearing. She had on a flower crown made of twigs and moss and a long flowing dress."

Alison doesn't remember exactly what he was wearing, but she recalls, "He brought a turkey to the party and he seemed really mellow and sweet. He was playing with the kids and their balloons and balls, and I remember thinking, What a neat guy."

Soon after that, they did what many men and women do in Hailey when they're interested in each other. They stayed outside as along as possible in the evening, hoping to bump into each other. Hailey is practically like a college campus that way. Eventually, you will run into whomever you happen to be looking for. "I'd ride my bike back and forth down the road just to see if Alison was around," Peter said.

Alison added, "And when I came home from work, I'd drive by his house, hoping to see him."

Often, you don't even have to ask someone out on a date in Hailey—you can just count on bumping into them or in the aisles of the supermarket or in the library, which looks like a tiny used bookstore. Alison and Pete "dated" in that way for a while, getting to know each other here and there, on the sidewalk, at various potluck dinners, or at slide shows given by mutual friends just back from traveling to some far-off exotic location.

"Then one night, he asked me to go see a band, Norton Buffalo," Alison said. "We left as friends and came back as something else. After the concert, we went to the hot springs out Deer Creek Road, a funky old enclosed concrete pool. It was a full moon and it was winter, so there was lots of snow and there were all these crystals on the snow like blue sparkles everywhere."

In Hailey, when anyone falls seriously in love, has a baby, or returns from a mountain-climbing expedition, almost everyone hears about it, often within hours. News about love travels especially fast. Hailey is filled with young couples carrying babies in backpacks—one resident calls it the "groovy little couples town"—and almost everyone welcomes and celebrates new love as much as new snow.

"This is a small town, and you somehow meet everyone," said Salome Taylor, a horticulturist and Hailey mom. "The first time I met Alison and Pete, they were on their bikes. They were riding one way, I was riding another, and I saw Alison's red hair. A good friend of mine who knew Pete told me he had fallen madly in love with this redheaded woman. So I stopped them and said, 'Hi, I'm Salome and you must be Pete and you must be the woman he's madly in love with.'"

All over Hailey, Alison is known as the redheaded woman. The midwife in Hailey, Pamela Plowman, describes her this way: "She's just this gorgeous, red-hair-down-to-her-waist flower fairy."

In Hailey, news travels quickly not only about new love but also about couples in trouble. I live in New York, where everything from the amount of your mortgage payments to the condition of your love life is superprivate. Those are things you'd have to be hypnotized to reveal. But in Hailey, people seem to know *everything* about each other's relationships. It's a town full of heart-to-heart talks. They're going on everywhere, in cafés, living rooms, on chairlifts and toboggans. When I interviewed Alison and Pete, they sat at a picnic table in their backyard, where there are no fences separating them from their neighbors. You can see right into other people's gardens; you can see what they're growing and hear everything they're saying. As Alison and Pete talked about their relationship, even about their problems, they didn't lower their voices or suggest going inside. They let their words float into the other yards like dandelion seeds, as if everyone knew about their private life anyway. Hailey is a town that seems to be on a mission to talk about love openly. It's the opposite of a 1950s small town where couples who wanted to discuss their relationship would pull their shades down and put on loud music. The people I met in Hailey seemed to really want their marriages and their neighbors' marriages to last, the way they hope the snow lasts as long as possible every spring.

"People in Hailey definitely make an effort to support one another's relationships," Alison said. "I feel I can call people up if I'm really struggling. I can say, 'This is my problem. Do you have any advice?' I appreciate that because when I'm going through hard times, I need other people. Otherwise, I feel too alone. I need to hear, 'This happened to us. You'll get through it.'"

In the summer of 1995, Alison and Peter announced to the community that they were engaged. Both had wanted to marry each other for a long time, but they hadn't been able to agree on the question of who was going to propose to whom. "I was waiting for him to do an old-fashioned proposal and get down on his knees, and he said, 'I want a feminist proposal' and was waiting for me to ask," Alison said.

Finally, they asked each other. While standing next to a jewelry booth at an arts fair in town, surrounded by people. "We said, 'Well, should we do it?' and we both looked at each other with a panicked look on our faces," Alison remembers. "I said, 'I don't know if I can make this decision until we eat lunch. So we went and sat next to a pond under a big tree and we just talked about it. Finally, he said, 'I really want to marry you,' and I said, 'Well, I really want to marry you.'"

Like most summertime parties in Hailey, their June 29, 1996, wedding was out-of-doors, potluck, inexpensive, and communal in every way. Everyone hoped it wouldn't rain, and it didn't.

Getting married outside was important to Alison and Pete. After all, she has the looks and serene temperament of someone who lives in a wildflower meadow, and Pete spends all of his free time either kayaking or telemark skiing. But even more important, they wanted to be married on *public* land, surrounded by communally owned mountains, meadows, aspen trees, and sagebrush.

"We wanted to be married on public land because it's everyone's land, it belongs to us," said Alison, who added that their one other requirement was that they marry near a roaring creek. "Instead of people looking around at a nice estate, they can look around and say, 'Wow, this is ours.'"

Alison and Peter reserved a buttercup meadow for their wedding, near a creek and an aspen grove at the base of the Boulder Mountains outside Sun Valley. The day before the wedding, it looked like a barn raising was happening there. As lavender butterflies flew around, the couple, along with their parents, sisters, brothers, ski partners, and sledding buddies, was busy erecting a white tent, which had been transported to the site all rolled up in the back of a friend's Pepto Bismol–pink pickup truck.

After the tent was up, friends continued to work, clearing the ground of nettles as sharp as fish hooks or decorating the dinner tables with gray-green, sagebrush-colored tablecloths. The bride's best girlfriends arrived with bunches of wildflowers—they'd gone door-to-door in Hailey, picking flowers from gardens and window boxes. Friends who owned a rug store in Hailey showed up with several Nepalese and Tibetan rugs to decorate the space. And two horsewomen who worked on a local ranch lent Alison and Peter hay bales for seating during the ceremony.

"Every once in a while I'd look up and say, 'Wow, this is really coming together,'" Peter said. "In the morning, there was just a pile of stuff in the meadow, and by the afternoon, there was this little beautiful world we'd created."

On the day of the wedding, guests arrived in the meadow with their dogs and children, wearing everything from flowered dresses and cowboy boots to blue jeans so faded they looked like they'd been treated in whitewater rapids. Some guests arrived by bicycle and simply laid their bikes down in the high grass. Others carried tents and sleeping bags and began setting up campsites so they could spend the night. Everyone brought plates of homemade food for the potluck reception.

One guest, Christy Bolton, described the crowd this way: "They are people definitely outside the corporate nine-to-five world who are willing to patch together all kinds of different jobs so they can live here. There are waiters, gardeners, painters, small shopkeepers, whitewater guides, people who lead mountain climbing trips to Nepal, nurses."

Laura Silber, Alison's sledding partner, was also there. She supported herself in Hailey by doing everything from standup comedy to quiltmaking to designing fleece skiwear. For a while she earned money cutting hair on a milk crate set up on the sidewalk in town. She even worked briefly as the personal chef for the actress Demi Moore. "I grew up in a standard middle-class family in Tupperware suburbia with my little red bike," Laura said. "I thought everybody got married and got jobs by the time they were twenty-five. And then when I was fifteen, I was riding on a train to Memphis and I sat next to a woman who was a wardrobe designer for Van Halen and I thought, Oh my God, I don't have to be an attorney or have a normal job. I can do all these weird things and travel around and make a living, a good living. So that's what I do."

Another friend, Salome Taylor, had just sold her family car, a vintage VW bus, on the Internet. Describing how she and her husband landed in Hailey, Salome said, "Here we are, two ex-yuppies, graduated from college in the mid-eighties, had professional careers in California, got fed up with it, split, traveled around Europe, came back, and ended up here. And we started meeting so many people like us, in their late twenties and early thirties, looking for a better lifestyle without two of us having to work and raise a family at the same time. It's an incredible lifestyle. We wouldn't trade it in for oceanfront California."

For the ceremony, the Tibetan rugs were laid out in the middle of the buttercup meadow, with hay bales piled up around them like straw bleachers. As the guests gathered together, the bride got dressed in a small white wedding trailer set up in the trees. The trailer was camouflaged with twigs, leaves, and green blankets and blended into the woods like a giant bird's nest. Everyone congregated around a homemade altar made out of sagebrush, perennial flowers (Alison and Pete later transplanted them into their backyard garden), and willow sticks collected by friends. "There are lots of weeping willow trees in our neighborhood park," Alison said. "So I told my friends, 'Here are some clippers. Go to the park and cut down some weeping willow branches.'"

Led by a flute player, the bride walked out of the woods accompanied by her closest community—her parents and two sisters, one carrying a baby, all holding hands and forming a line as wide as a river. Alison wore a silk shantung empire-style dress sewn by one sister, Holly, and a wreath made out of wildflowers collected by friends from nearby canyons and other public lands. The bridegroom, who walked out of the woods with his family, dressed in the colors of a hayfield—straw-colored cotton pants, a slightly darker vest, and a collarless white shirt. Like the bride, he was barefoot.

The couple was married with friends and snowcapped mountains surrounding them, as dogs ran through the meadow and wind shook the aspen leaves so they jiggled like charms on a bracelet.

Throughout the ceremony, the community contributed. At various times, friends stood up and played guitar, read poetry, or reminisced about trips to Tibet or Morocco with

Pete. At one point, the bridegroom's grandfather stood and welcomed Alison into the family. "Peter is my first grandson, but he's not the first one to get married," he said. "We've been waiting a long time for this." Then, turning to the bride, he added, "Mrs. Free Spirit, all the luck."

The couple wrote their own vows, which covered everything from how marriage goes through changing seasons to why they were so crazy about each other. "I honor the way you wear dirt in the garden with the same grace that you wear this dress," Pete told Alison as part of his vows. "I honor you for your physical beauty, which takes my breath away, and for your inner beauty and strength, which also take my breath away. I could live without you, but I don't want to."

Instead of rings, Alison and Pete exchanged matching silver pendants they had chosen together, bought for each other, and worn for several months before the wedding as a way of imbuing them with their thoughts, love, and overall good vibes. "I made a definite point of wearing my pendant if I was doing something big," Pete said. "I wore it whenever I went backcountry skiing or when I spent four days alone in the desert."

Alison added, "When we were fighting, we would take them off."

The wedding was officiated by Lea Reed, a nondenominational minister who ended the ceremony by asking all of the guests to gather closely around the couple and hold hands. "Move in as close as you can," she said. "Anyone who has been married knows how important it is to be held by your community." Even the consecration of the marriage was a group effort. As everyone held hands, hugged, and crowded around the couple, Lea said, "In the name of community and with the love and support of all these faces you see before you, we all joyfully pronounce you lifetime partners."

Afterward, everyone gathered under the big tent for a potluck meal. Friends of the couple acted as waiters, serving everything from salmon to sesame noodles to homemade bread, out of containers ranging from heirloom silver bowls to handpainted ceramic ones to Tupperware. The tiramisu wedding cake was made by the bride and covered with leaves, berries, and flowers—it looked like it had been sitting in the forest for the day.

"When you go to a catered wedding, you're disconnected from the food," Peter said. "At a potluck, there's an incredible feeling of love and connectedness. Also, it adds a dimension of mystery to the wedding. We had no idea what people would bring; we just trusted they would bring something great."

For everyone, the idea of a potluck—the mismatched dishes, the no-frills philosophy, the group effort—really reflected the way they want to live, in a group made up of people depending on each other and all bringing something to the table. "An outdoor potluck wedding is the best kind you can have," said Laura Silber. "You have muddy dogs, you have guests staying in tents. The kids are part of it, and they're allowed to run around. Everyone can get dirty. The food is all homemade by the guests. It's about community and marriage, not about the money that went into it."

Whether it was the food or the sunlight, which cast a honeysuckle-yellow glow on everything, the community that gathered under the tent that evening did seem unusually connected and close. The guests even provided the music—an open invitation jam session went on all night, long after most of the guests had headed back to their trucks and tents.

Many of the people at Alison and Pete's wedding had seen each other marry, plant gardens, start businesses, build houses, and give birth. Pamela Plowman, Hailey's midwife, looked around at the crowd and said she'd delivered every single child at the wedding, most of them at home.

"More and more, births in Hailey are developing into a woman's community activity," she said. "When women have babies now, they attend each other's births in groups, and afterward, there are dinner deliveries arriving on the doorstep for weeks. The community is hugely supportive of relationships and families. We're all here to grow, and marriage is the ultimate growth experience." She added that once you become a "Hailey couple," everyone in town crosses their fingers for you and hopes.

While some couples arrive in Hailey without knowing anyone, carrying their skis and one duffel bag, with a hundred or so dollars in their pocket, this is a very easy town to settle down in. Unlike being a couple in the city, being a couple in Hailey means leaving your door unlocked in every sense of the word. Alison and Pete are an official Hailey couple now. When their car is snowed in, friends come over and dig it out. When their house needs painting, neighbors show up. When they are fighting or having problems in their relationship, friends take them for walks in the mountains and offer advice. "I've watched how easy it is for couples to fall apart," Alison said. "Living here is a great safety net against that."

On March 11, 1998, Pete and Alison had a baby girl, Riley. Like many moms in Hailey, Alison gave birth at home with Pamela, the midwife. During her twenty-hour labor, Alison was surrounded by Pete and their best friends. Word spread quickly once she had given birth. "Within a half hour after I had Riley, a friend saw Pamela's car here—it says 'midwife' on it—and she just came in and brought me plum juice and some honey," Alison said. "For weeks afterward, people came over to clean up or do some laundry or put tons of groceries in the fridge or drop off meals. We got lots of lasagna."

Already, Riley has a small community of peers around her. Three children were born in the neighborhood during the month of March, and all of them started life with home-made meals on their doorstep. Alison and Pete, like many of their friends in Hailey, share their relationship and family life with the community just as happily as they share ski wax or photographs from faraway trips or cooking responsibilities at parties or tips on how to repair mountain bike tires Their community wedding was so much more romantic than two people running off and eloping together—

their wedding tent that night was surrounded by little tents and campfires like a ring of covered wagons safeguarding them. Alison and Pete taught me that while two people may be able to create a comfortable cocoon, a community like theirs offers much greater security against everything from bad snowstorms to broken hearts. You lose some privacy, but you gain an incredible amount of protection—not to mention homemade food.

I once met a couple, Helen Hiebert and Ted Katauskas, who lived in a communal house in Brooklyn, New York, with six roommates and a bathtub full of flowers in the front yard. Helen, Ted, and their roommates shared everything from the rent to interior decorating decisions to refrigerator space to household chores. "My chores are paying bills, balancing the checkbook, and cobweb control," Helen told me. She also said that in some ways, a communal home taught her the basics about what love really is—it's about cooperation, carrying your own load and sometimes taking on the load of others, sharing chores, knowing that others are dependent on you, and being the sort of person who comes through when needed. Living in a communal town like Hailey is not as extreme as a cooperative house, but the same lessons about love and sharing are in the air.

The other day, I was driving my three-year-old son home from school. He was sitting in the backseat, as quiet as an owl on the branch of a tree. I told him I'd give him a dollar for his thoughts. (When I was growing up, my mother used to say, "Penny for your thoughts?" but my son has no respect for pennies.) He looked at me solemnly and said, "Mom, my thoughts are a secret."

We are born secretive, I think, but what I learned from Alison and Pete is that in many ways, love works best, and may even have a better chance of lasting, when your inner life is not so private, when you leave your doors and everything else unlocked.

Diehard Bachelor

Meets Single

Mom

SOME PEOPLE THINK that when they're look-
ing for love, they should look for someone exactly like
themselves. But before they met, Susan Stevenson and Rick
Woodward led such different lives that one friend of theirs
said the leap between their worlds was "of the Jesse Owens
ilk."

Susan lives on Park Avenue in New York City, in a gigantic apartment. It is so big that adults with a good sense
of direction regularly get lost in it. The apartment, like Susan herself, comes on strong. The living room is as cheerful
and bright as an Easter dress, decorated in hot pinks,
lemonade yellows, and lime greens, full of polka dots and
stripes. Throughout the place, there's constant activity and
noise. Susan, a divorced mom in her forties, has four
teenage children—Mary, Josephine, Gordon, and Scott—

one tiny white dog, one room full of Nintendo games, and six telephone lines, each with a different ring. "I have a switchboard here," Susan said. "Each kid has a line and I have two. I had to wise up to this. Why would anyone answer a teenager's phone if they didn't have to?"

Before meeting Rick, Susan rarely went out on dates with men. For one thing, she could never be reached on the telephone by anyone, friends or otherwise, who might want to ask her out. One of her children or her children's best friends invariably answered and tended to hang up immediately if it wasn't for them. Also, Susan was never awake late enough to go out with an adult—she went to sleep at 9 P.M. sharp and got up around 6. Plus, she preferred to stay home doing homework with her kids rather than getting dressed up and going out on dates that generally put her to sleep. "My version of dating was I had to take care of my children come hell or high water and everything else came later," she said.

If she ever went out in the evening, it was usually to one of her children's school plays, concerts, Halloween parties, or class meetings. She often sat alone, in a tiny chair built for children rather than adults, surrounded by still-married parents. "It was very difficult to be a single mom," she said. "I basically don't think people are nice to single moms. They think single moms are dangerous. I felt isolated, in certain ways shunned."

The only Valentine's Day cards she received were from the kids—homemade cards hung in one corner of her kitchen like a string of red peppers.

On the rare occasions that she did go out with a man, her entourage—which Susan describes as "bigger than Don King's"—soon scared him away. Spending a weekend with Susan usually means piling into her bright red Cherokee Jeep with the dog, the hockey equipment, the kids, and the kids' friends, and driving out to Southampton, Long Island. She has a country house there filled with sea air and the sound of teenagers running around like squirrels in an attic. "As a single parent with four young children, I thought no one would want to go out with me," she said. "But I was wrong."

Susan met Rick Woodward four years ago when they were introduced by a mutual friend at the opening of an art show. "She came on pretty strong," he recalls. "I had to take a few steps back because Susan is very direct. She's a forceful personality."

Rick's life at the time was so different from hers that they weren't even awake for many of the same hours. He was a longtime bachelor who went out on a date almost every night, to gallery openings, jazz concerts, black-tie dinners, movie premieres, and book parties.

Sometimes, two or three women thought they were his steady girlfriend at the same time. His answering machine almost always contained messages from women who began by simply saying, "Hi," in that familiar "we're a couple and I don't have to say who I am" tone of voice. Around Valentine's Day, he received as many cards as most people do at Christmastime.

In her Southampton kitchen, Susan had two giant refrigerators, both always so full that opening either of them was like winning at a slot machine—apples, oranges, cupcakes, and Coke cans poured out. Rick's refrigerator was an entirely different story. It was perpetually empty, a forlorn sight. There are certain things that are guaranteed to depress you, like looking back through your high school yearbook the year no one asked you to the prom. For Rick, peering in his refrigerator was like that. There was nothing in there except a bottle of ketchup so old it was harder to open than a childproof container of aspirin.

"Basically, only one person could stand in my kitchen," he said. "And the refrigerator was filled with all kinds of condiments with nothing to put the condiments on."

A freelance writer in his forties who covers the photography, art, and music scene, Rick lived on the Upper West Side, across Central Park from Susan. While Susan's apartment was filled with sunlight that evoked California and turquoise swimming pools, Rick's was dark and moody. "His apartment is one of those Upper West Side apartments with sixty-five coats of paint, lots of books, and no light," said Chris Calhoun, a literary agent and an old friend of Rick's. "It's filled with very cool black-and-white photos, and those are the most colorful things in the room. His apartment windows have been painted closed. Even if he had a view, you couldn't see it."

Like their apartments, Susan and Rick have totally different temperaments. She's talkative, funny, busy, bossy, and outspoken. "If my mom could be a color, she'd be fire engine red," said Josephine Stevenson, one of Susan's daughters.

Mickey Lyons, an old friend of Susan's, described her this way: "Susan is perfectly comfortable with ten guys in a room. She can handle herself fine. Then she can walk into a room with a bunch of her girlfriends and do the same thing. She can cross the line from Mars to Venus."

Friends describe Rick as far quieter and subtler than Susan: "He was always impressively mysterious," said Michael Tomasky, a fellow writer. "He's got this cool, aloof manner. He's a man of few words, well-chosen ones."

Although Rick went out almost every night and Susan almost never, the one thing they did have in common was this: love lives with a modern kind of malaise about them. Both had been through long relationships that were like tap water—no longer healthy but not yet deadly, either.

"I went out with one woman for about five years," Rick said. "She moved from New Mexico to New York, and it didn't work out because of real estate more than anything else. I was not used to sharing space with anyone, and my books took up three-fourths of the apartment and I wasn't willing to cede to her clothes. I was an idiot in that department. That was as close as I'd come to getting married. To get back at me, she decided her father should get her a NordicTrack, which she put in the middle of my study. There really wasn't enough space for the two of us and my books and the NordicTrack. Finally, I got the message and I carted off five hundred books and put them in storage, but by that time, the relationship just wasn't working."

Among friends, Rick became known as "a chick magnet" and a diehard bachelor—someone who was handsome, smart, rumpled, and a disaster when it came to love. Watching the course of his relationships was like sitting through bad experimental films—after a while even he, and many of his friends, couldn't wait for them to end. Nevertheless, Rick honestly hoped he'd marry one day. "For years, I wanted to get married and have children," he said. "There are friends of mine who are not the marrying kind, but I was. I tended to be fairly monogamous, and the idea of forever was appealing to me, of finding someone you might actually want to grow old with." When he thought about settling down, he saw himself in a bohemian marriage, living in a small Brooklyn flat with a rundown country cottage in the Catskill mountains, a beat-up old car, books everywhere, and jazz playing in the background.

The night they met at the art show opening, Susan and Rick liked each other right away, although they didn't talk for very long. "He was with a really gorgeous date, oh boy," she said. "We spoke for a while, and then he said he had to get back to this other woman."

Rick remembers wishing he didn't have a date that night. "Oh, I thought Susan was very attractive," he said. "She didn't hold back in the least. She wasn't coy at all, and I was not used to that. Everyone knows immediately how Susan feels about them. What you see is what you get. Susan will tell you right away where she went to school and where she bought the dress she's wearing and how much it cost. She will give you advice on almost any topic, and she will find a way to connect her life to yours in a hurry. And she has an encyclopedic range of references and friends and places she's been. She'll tell you about her children. Susan is the most unusual combination of hard and soft I've ever met. She's very sentimental about dogs and babies, but she's also a completely take-no-prisoners negotiator. I'd never met a woman who was anything like her."

The week after they met, Rick tried calling Susan several times but recalls it was like attempting to reach someone in a college dorm during the last week of school. "Three or four people would always get on the line," he said. He finally got through to her by pretending to be a telephone company representative calling with an emergency. She picked up and, screaming over all the background noise, she agreed to meet him for a drink. A few nights later, they got together at 10 P.M., after her kids were asleep, in a hotel bar a few blocks from her apartment.

Susan made up her mind about Rick fast, partly because she wanted to get home to the kids and partly because that's how she is, a blunt, decisive, and confident person. "We had a drink and that was it for me," she said. "I felt like I'd been through a lot and you have to trust your instincts. With Rick, I just felt it was the right thing. I was really turned on by him, and I thought he was an amazing man, very complete and well spoken and honest and sure of himself but kind. I felt it was different, it was kind of magical. So, I went with it. I'm not a particularly cautious person."

The first time Rick spent the night with Susan, he couldn't find his way out of her apartment in the morning.

"When I woke up, I remember being in this huge bedroom and there was Susan followed by the dog marching out the door to wake the children up," he remembered. "Then she got the children out and she went to exercise class, and I took a wrong turn and I actually got lost in her apartment. I really didn't know where I was, there were so many rooms."

After that, a few evenings a week, he would walk from his apartment across Central Park to have dinner with the Stevenson family in their enormous, loud, cheerful kitchen. He says at first he was drawn across the park mostly by curiosity—he wanted to learn about this unfamiliar, homey life on the other side of Manhattan. "I couldn't imagine ever being part of Susan's world," he said. "It was more like I was doing investigative reporting."

When Rick talked to friends about Susan, he described their relationship as crazy and fun but doomed. He was certain it wouldn't last very long. "The first two weeks were just sort of a lark," he recalls. "She was a woman who had four kids and a little white dog! That seemed like a deal breaker. Then I contracted the flu and she came over on a mission of mercy to take care of me. She brought flowers, cookies, chicken soup, a little grocery sack full of things to make me feel better. At that point, I thought, Boy, this is pretty wonderful, to instantly have a family. There's nothing worse than being single and sick. I thought, Am I actually going to be sixty years old and living like this?"

Before long, Rick was spending weekends in Susan's overloaded, bright red Jeep and driving out to the country with carsick children rather than hanging out in downtown jazz clubs and flirting with women. "I remember the first time we picked the kids up at school to drive out to Southampton for the weekend," he said. "They were like little quiet monkeys, staring at me and trying to figure me out. Susan was so wonderfully cool about the whole thing, as if this was the most natural thing in the world. I guess she had put them on warning that she didn't want them to blow it this time because it was serious."

Rick thought making friends with Susan's kids would be more difficult than befriending supermodels or Secret Service agents, but it turned out he was wrong. According to Susan, her kids approved of him right away, thinking he was cool, smart, and also useful. "My kids really liked Rick," Susan said. "He knows all the answers to Jeopardy. He corrects the grammar in their homework. He makes an effort to talk to them every day and they trust his advice. He never misses their basketball games. Who knew? Who would ever guess this longtime bachelor would be so good at fatherhood?"

Rick and Susan's courtship was definitely family oriented—they fell in love in the bleachers at her kids' soccer games, in the small theaters where school plays are held, in the TV room at home. "It was home-based dating," Rick said. "Recently, I was walking to Susan's apartment and I remember thinking, Mary will be making cookies and Susan will be making dinner. There will be all this domestic activity and a warm, good-smelling kitchen. And I must say the little white dog I thought I could not tolerate, the little bichon frise, turned out to be my best friend."

Susan adjusted well to Rick's very different world, too, partly because she is the sort of person who never fell in love with anyone remotely similar to her. "I'm good at accepting people for who they are," she said. "I'm a twin. I don't want to be with a person just like me or who does things just like I do."

When they met, both she and Rick had summer houses near the ocean on Long Island, but like their apartments, they were very different places. Hers was in Southampton, a big shingle-style house with room after room full of pretty couches and beautiful antiques, while his was a dark little shack in Wainscott that he shared with his friend and fellow bachelor Chris Calhoun. It was so full of insects, they called it The Dead Bugs Society.

"Our house was dilapidated, a dump compared to her castle in Southampton," Chris said. "But Susan did a wonderful thing—when she rented out her house for August, we invited her to our house, where parts of the floors were falling in and there were rusty cabinets in the kitchen and moldy blankets. I thought she would be scared away and never want to see Rick again, but she arrived with a bag of groceries, a quart of vodka, lots of great snacks, and three bouquets of flowers. That's when I knew that they would get married. She'll rock with anything."

For a long time, even after they had fallen in love, marriage was the last thing on Susan and Rick's minds. Neither could really imagine becoming husband and wife. In fact, after they had been dating for several months and he knew her apartment so well he no longer got lost in it, Susan announced to him one night that she would never, never, never remarry. "I told all of my friends to smack me if I ever thought of getting married again," Susan said. "I was the one who wanted to stay with my first husband, and that didn't work out. Splitting up was horrible, and I didn't want to ever go through it again, though of course it's like having a baby. Now, I can't remember how terrible it was."

She added, "But after a while, when I thought about marrying Rick, there was a part of me that said, 'Go for it.'"

In the end, Susan decided to marry Rick for unglamorous, down-to-earth reasons—because he was a guy she liked reading the newspaper with, because he was great company at the breakfast table and in the car on long drives. Like many people I've met who have been married before, Susan wasn't looking for the kind of love that's so exciting it gives you insomnia and temporary eating disorders, she was looking for someone she would love hanging out with on the living room couch all Saturday afternoon—not that she ever has time to do that. "I wanted a man I could live with as I got older," she said. "It was much different than my first marriage. Who thinks about growing old with somebody the first time? But that's what marriage is all about. It's about talking to each other and reading books and doing all the mundane things of life together."

At the end of their first year of dating, Rick and Susan were walking through Tiffany's at Christmastime. "I thought

I was just buying her some earrings, and she went right to the ring counter," Rick remembers. "She had liked this one ring and she took me to it, and we bought it and I realized I was engaged. It's typical that Susan would take charge like that."

On Sunday, April 20, 1997, as the telephones rang constantly in the background, they were married in her sprawling apartment. Although the wedding took place inside, it felt like a garden wedding. Rick and Susan said their vows in the living room, surrounded by couches upholstered in flowery chintz material and hot pink chairs with tiny chartreuse polka dots. Sunlight the color of chamomile tea poured in the windows.

The bride's two daughters, Mary and Josephine, acted as her bridesmaids. They were dressed in spring colors—one chose pale blue, the other lime green with an empire waistband made out of yellow fabric daisies. The little white dog who has become Rick's best friend was there, wearing a chartreuse collar and smelling of perfumed shampoo. A collection of turquoise glass pitchers containing fuchsia peonies were lined up on a mantelpiece. Another row of vases, tiny ones tied with French ribbons and containing miniature pink roses with buds the size of marbles, decorated the top of a gilded mirror. In his whole life, Rick had never stood in a room with so many flowers, breakable little vases, and beautifully tied ribbons.

The wedding, like the couple's courtship, was a family affair. Josephine chose the cake; Mary was the wedding's official photographer; and the day before the wedding,

Susan's two sons were busy cutting out pink paper hearts to throw on the couple immediately after the ceremony. As soon as the boys tossed them, and the lime green rug was completely covered with pink hearts, they asked if they could go play Nintendo for a while. Meanwhile, Josephine stood in the hallway, talking about her mom and Rick—in her opinion, they were truly in love but still pretty uncool. "They do old people stuff," she said. "They do the crossword together and listen to jazz music. They talk about art. Fuddy-duddy stuff."

There were only about thirty people invited to the ceremony, but later in the day, Rick and Susan hosted a champagne and hors d'oeuvres reception for nearly 150 people in the apartment. In the crowd, there was a mix of journalists in crumpled khakis and socialites in hot pink Chanel suits and Cartier watches—Rick's friends and Susan's friends. Many seemed genuinely moved by the story of a longtime, rather stern and distant bachelor finding love with a frenetic, exhausted mother of four.

"Rick was a major literary bachelor," said Ilene Rosenzweig, one of the journalists among the guests. "He was unattainable in that mysterious way the modern bachelor is. Then, lo and behold, I saw Rick at a party one night, and Susan was sitting on his lap with her arm around him and she looked very much like she had proprietary rights. You wonder what becomes of these bachelor guys past forty, but he really figured it out; he fell in love and found this fabulous family. He had it better figured out than we all suspected."

Even at the wedding, Rick still seemed shocked to have fallen in love with a mother of four who lived in an apartment with wraparound terraces overlooking Park Avenue. "Before meeting Susan, I never even knew anybody who lived on the Upper East Side," he said.

If you had asked him at any point in his life to describe the kind of woman he wanted to spend his life with, he might have described a deep, soulful philosophy major, a downtown artist, a nocturnal jazz musician, a sensitive poet—but never an uptown, harried, earthy, wealthy, fast-talking mom. "I could never have imagined this," he said. "When I was eighteen, I thought I was going to be teaching philosophy and living in a hut in Scotland. I imagined I'd be far, far from here."

WHILE WRITING my column, the best love stories I've heard usually contain that element of the totally unexpected. One bride I met was a filmmaker who always imagined she would marry another filmmaker or an actor, someone she met on a movie set. But she fell in love with an unemployed man in a wheelchair whom she encountered in a thirty-something chat room on the Internet. Similarly, I once interviewed a high-powered Washington career woman in her forties who figured she would marry an older congressman or senator, never have children, and live an intense, work-oriented life in Washington. Instead, she fell in love with a single father who had four children, a lawyer who was recently named ambassador to Portugal. Now she is living in the American embassy in Lisbon, far from Washington and all its cocktail parties and intense debate. She no longer works; she is an ambassador's wife and a stepmother, surrounded by chauffeurs, children, and seating charts for dinner parties. Describing how she adjusted to her new domestic life, she said, "It was total immersion. I'm a terrible cook. I can cook enough to keep these kids alive, but that's about it."

In some ways, falling in love can be like getting on the wrong airplane and landing in Paris when you thought you were headed for Newark, New Jersey—or the other way around. It can take you places you never imagined, turn you from a secretary into a scuba diver, an apartment dweller into a person living on a sailboat, a lifelong bachelor like Rick into a stepfather trying to teach four teenagers to appreciate jazz. When people ask me for love advice, I always tell them: Don't look for a certain kind of person, a lawyer or a high-fashion model or an Ivy League tennis player. It's possible that you may find them, but not find love. Instead, just look for a feeling. When it comes to love, as with kissing, it's best to close your eyes. As Susan said, "You can't look for the perfect partner, whatever you think that is. You have to be open to whoever's out there, and they show up in the strangest places most of the time."

AT RICK AND Susan's wedding reception, a few men in the crowd were talking about whether they would ever get involved with a woman who had as large and as loud an entourage as the bride's. "I'd run like hell," said one man.

Another, Barry Cooper, said, "At forty-four, Rick has gone from being a bachelor to a stepfather of four. He's braver than I am. On paper, this might not be the most rational, logical thing to do, but I think it's proof that love exists."

About a year after the wedding, I called Rick on the telephone. He seemed almost completely transformed into a mellow family man. Almost all traces of the impatient bachelor, the man with a short attention span for almost everything, but especially for relationships, were gone. "In the past, I was so quick to declare a relationship—love—over and done with after one or a series of fights," he said. "That's just the way it was. But now, every time I've thought I couldn't continue in this any longer, a day later I'm happy as a clam. So, I'm thinking long-term in every respect of my life. That's something I never used to do. When I was in college, if a woman couldn't discuss *Ulysses*, that was it. She was unworthy of conversing with. Now, I can fight with Susan and blow up and I know twelve hours later it will be forgotten."

When he first met Susan, Rick never thought he could fall seriously in love with a single mom who had four kids and a tiny, white, fluffy dog who looks like a disheveled roll of toilet paper. But now, Susan's motherliness, her cooking, her enormous overflowing refrigerators, and her fierce family loyalty are among the things he loves most about her.

"As much as a hothead as she is, Susan is one of the most loyal people I've ever met," Rick said. "She's steadfast, and a lot of that has to do with her being a mother of four children. She just can't up and walk away like single men and women can. It's great when you know you're with someone who has that kind of stamina and that kind of loyalty and goodness. You could say I fell in love watching her as a mom. She's also a very sexy babe."

The Ultimate

Adventure

IN MANY WAYS, Mel Schneeberger seems like a woman you might meet in a Hemingway novel. She is beautiful, with blond hair and eyes the color of Coca-Cola, an athletic woman who looks great in ski pants, jodhpurs, and tennis whites. She fly-fishes, mountain-climbs and skis, and she wears hiking boots most of the time, even with business suits. An attorney in her late twenties, she has the firm handshake and great pool game of a hard-boiled detective. When she drives her car, loud music is always playing. She drinks bourbon, and her closet is filled with jeans and men's white T-shirts. Her favorite words, besides swear words, are *awesome* and *adventurous.*

While she has a tough, shoot-from-the-hip personality, she also has a very feminine, swanlike side. "She's a woman full of surprises," said Mo Hanson, a close friend of Mel's.

"She'll hike ten miles with blisters all over her feet and fly-fish in hailstorms, yet she willingly admits to loving manicures."

When she's in the wilderness, Mel is not afraid of much. She often goes hiking in Alaska, venturing deep into the woods alone, carrying a rifle in case she meets any bears. In life, especially in her love life, she's the same way. Nothing scares her, not the possibility of heartbreak, not loneliness, especially not rejection. When it comes to love (and bears), I have never met anyone so gutsy. She would not hesitate to call a man and ask him out or lay her cards out on the table, clear as stars in a Colorado sky, and let a man know exactly how she felt about him.

While Mel always imagined she would find the love of her life in the middle of a trout stream or while rappelling down a rock face, she met Chris Robbins at a black-tie party in 1994 in New York City, where they were both living at the time. She remembers being bored at the party and tired of city life in general. She was thinking of crystal clear Idaho streams and river pebbles for most of the night and was dying to get out of her tight gown and into a pair of baggy jeans. Around midnight, she walked up to the bar to order a bourbon on the rocks, which she planned to carry with her on the cab ride home. While she was standing there stirring the ice in her drink, about to run out of the party, Chris walked up behind her and said, "God, that looks good. I'll have one, too."

Chris is in his twenties and, like Mel, he's outdoorsy, rugged, and elegant at once, the sort of guy who RollerBlades to work in beautifully tailored suits. Standing at the bar with their bourbons, he and Mel hit it off right away. "We spoke for about ten minutes, and I was so struck by our similarities," Mel remembers. "We were immediately talking about our love for the outdoors. We exchanged phone numbers, and when I got home at two A.M., I picked up the phone and called him. I left a message on his machine: 'Hi, this is Mel. I met you a half hour ago. Let's go for a run in the morning.' I hung up and my roommate screamed at me. She said, 'He's going to think this is fatal attraction!'"

In fact, Chris was impressed rather than terrified by Mel's middle-of-the-night call. Like her, he enjoys being on the edge and taking risks. He doesn't mind sleeping in snow caves or in a sleeping bag tied to the side of a rock face like a cocoon—actually, he prefers such accommodations to luxury hotels. He is the sort of person who loves exposure—exposure to the cold, exposure to extreme mountain climbing conditions, exposure to all kinds of people, exposure of the heart.

"I'm attracted to women who make decisions based on their gut and how they feel," he said. "I've always wanted to be with a woman like that rather than someone who might not make the call out of fear."

Mel taught me an important lesson—when it comes to love, don't chicken out or follow conventional rules. "Anyone who has read *Glamour* magazine knows that after you get someone's phone number, you have to wait a couple of days and not be overeager so he doesn't think you're desperate," said Catherine Sheehan, a lawyer who met Mel when they were students together at Dartmouth College. "Well, Mel got home from the party, and she had just met this wonderful man so she picked up the phone and left a message on his machine. Most guys would be spooked by that. But Chris and Mel are very able to follow their hearts and to take a risk."

UNLIKE MEL AND CHRIS, I am not a risk-taker by nature—I don't like driving fast, skiing out of bounds, throwing dinner parties, or sleeping outside. But I've interviewed so many people who risked everything from their job to their self-esteem to make love happen, like a woman who once walked up to a total stranger in a rainstorm, thinking he was incredibly handsome, and asked if he would like to share her umbrella.

A few years ago, I interviewed a minister's daughter from Ohio who met her future husband on the subway in New York. An English teacher, she was bookish and cautious and she never, ever talked to strangers. But one day, while she was traveling home on the F train, underlining passages in a Mark Twain novel, a tall, gregarious man approached her and attempted to start up a conversation. When she didn't respond, he took one of her clogs off. She was horrified, but also amused. There was something about this goofy, lanky guy that appealed to her as strongly as her favorite poems, so she started talking to him. When he invited her for a drink, she did something totally out of character: she got off the subway at his stop and walked with him to a dark nearby bar. Around midnight, he invited her back to his apartment to see his baseball card collection. She actually went.

Often, people fall in love the one time they take a risk like that—an unheard-of leap against reason, parental advice, your own character, rules of etiquette, and traditional dating wisdom. I've met incredibly shy people who because they sensed the possibility of love introduced themselves to someone on an airplane or sent a drink to a stranger across a bar. Love, like hiking in grizzly bear territory, sometimes requires much, much more guts than you think you have.

Several years ago, I interviewed Ruth Allen, a twenty-something woman who met Jonathan Cox in a ballroom dancing class. A formal, conservative person, Ruth reads Amy Vanderbilt, wears pearls, and gets dressed up for everything from lunch with her parents to airplane trips. She had never called a man for romantic reasons in her life. But one day in class, Jonathan handed her his card and asked her to phone him sometime. Even though he was a terrible dancer—he occasionally stepped on her toes when they danced together or turned her hand as if it were a doorknob—she had a mad crush on him. While they hardly ever spoke to each other in class, except to mutter "one, two, one, two" as they waltzed, she liked his bright blue eyes, his conservative pin-striped suits, his perfect haircut. So, she spent days gathering enough courage to dial his number.

"I was so nervous," she recalled. "We were strangers. All I knew about him was his name and what he looked like. Finally, I called and his secretary asked, 'May I tell him who's calling?' And I said, 'It's Ruth Allen from ballroom dancing class.' It was an exercise in total humiliation."

Calling someone you don't know well or showing up on the doorstep of an ex-boyfriend to say you miss him does sometimes feel like an exercise in total humiliation. A pilot once told me that falling in love is similar to "putting the nose down" on an airplane. When a plane is about to stall, putting the nose down can add enough forward power to get it going again. But it can also backfire and cause a crash. Still, it's wiser to put yourself in danger than to play it safe. "It's hazardous NOT to take the risk," the pilot told me. "In love and flying, you sometimes have to do the opposite of what's easy."

FROM THE VERY beginning, risk, challenge, and adventure have been the code words, the themes, and the operating principles of Chris and Mel's romance. Almost everything they do is bold, out of the ordinary, purposely different, even difficult. When Chris called Mel back the morning after her middle-of-the-night call, she picked up the phone on the first ring—Mel is not the kind of woman who hides demurely behind her answering machine or lets the phone ring six times before answering to show how busy or popular she is. And when she says hello, it's pleasantly loud, like wind chimes in a strong wind. After she and Chris talked for a while, they decided to get together that night for burritos, beer, and a game of pool.

As usual, Mel broke all the rules of dating that night, acting the opposite of hard-to-get, unavailable, or demure. "We met at my apartment first," Chris said. "I remember Mel was wearing jeans and boots and a white T-shirt. There was something very natural and forthright and straight about her. Before we left for dinner, she took a picture of herself out of her wallet and said, 'Well, you'll need this.' Then she put it on my bookshelf. Probably a lot of people would be amazed at the boldness of that, but I loved it."

Mel recalls that while they were walking to Benny's Burritos that night, she looked over at Chris and thought, Holy shit, this is the man I'm going to marry. While many people compare the moment of falling in love, the moment of "knowing," to a feeling that the earth is shifting, a thunderous experience, Mel said that she felt more like her ears were filled with cotton balls. She said it was as if New York City had become unnaturally quiet and everything was muffled and calm, like the morning after a heavy snowfall, when the streets are silent and at the same time totally transformed.

Over burritos, Chris was also thinking he wanted to marry Mel, but he didn't admit that until their third date, two nights later. "Our third date was the riskiest evening," Mel says. "We went to a French café and Chris was getting all teary-eyed, and I asked him if he was okay and he said, 'I'm actually wonderful.' He just kept looking at me, and then he said, 'I know you're the one. I found you.' And I said, 'I know what you mean. I feel like I found you, too.' I cried and he cried. It was just awesome."

Chris summed up their first week together this way: "We fell in love like bricks to the bottom of the ocean. We just plummeted."

They moved into a loft together a few months later, and exactly 364 days after they met, Chris proposed on the rooftop of their building. When he went to buy the ring, his credit card was declined, so he borrowed his brother's and then left a message on Mel's father's answering machine saying he couldn't wait any longer to propose to his daughter.

Just after they got engaged, I visited Chris and Mel in their loft, which used to be the artist Jackson Pollock's painting studio. Chris was wearing a chrome gray suit and RollerBlades (he'd just returned from work), while Mel arrived home from the office in a brown bell-bottom pantsuit and big, heavy hiking boots. Loud music played in the background, and Mel kept jumping up to turn it up even more, screaming, "You'll love this song!" She never sits still for long.

Their apartment was filled with Navajo rugs, heavy, Mission-style wood furniture the color of dark chocolate, and pictures of them together on the top of mountains, rafting down rapids, skiing steep, clifflike slopes. In their first year together, they had taken many adventures and experienced everything from frostbite to hail the size of crab apples. Mel says she knew Chris was the perfect man for her when they were camping in the backcountry of Idaho, in a blizzard, and Chris filled her sleeping bag one night with hot water bottles, making it feel like she was under an electric blanket.

While we spoke, Mel and Chris never called each other boyfriend or girlfriend; instead, they described themselves as "partners in adventure." As Mel poured two tall glasses of lemonade that matched her blond hair, she explained that she didn't want the usual, unadventurous things from a marriage—a sense of security and comfort, a two-car garage, a nice house with a leakproof roof and a thirty-year mortgage, the confidence that you can finish the other's sentences whenever necessary. Instead, she looked forward to lots of traveling with Chris, preferably without hotel reservations or clear plans; many changes of address; unsteady paychecks; unclear career paths; rough weather; and an overall feeling of instability, of hanging by their fingernails on a rock face.

"To us, adventure is very much about climbing mountains and telemark skiing together, but it's so much more about having an adventurous life," she said. "I am not at all interested in being comfortable. I always want to think, What's next? When you're comfortable, I think you stop living life with velocity. We're committed to having a life that's unpredictable. We're up for anything. We have no idea where we'll be in five years."

A year and a half after they met, Mel and Chris were married in North Muskegon, Michigan, at the bride's childhood home, a large gray house filled with artwork and pretty lamps. The house overlooks Bear Lake and is surrounded by tall evergreen trees shaped like enormous church spires.

The ceremony took place on the tennis court, where Chris and Mel's favorite songs blared from speakers hanging on the chain link fence. Guests were given tiny bottles of bubbles, which they blew all night, under a full moon. As a bride, Mel combined both her bold, nothing-scares-me personality and her feminine, swanlike side. She walked down the middle of the tennis court in a tight-fitting, classic gown with her toenails painted blue—for good luck— and bright red patent leather shoes. "I'm passionately in love with Chris, and the red shoes were this fun expression of how much I love the guy," she said.

On her head, she wore a thick wreath of red roses that were as bright as her shoes. "At first I was going to wear the flowers braided in my hair and go for the wood nymph look, the *Vogue*-slash-Outward Bound look, almost like I'd fallen off my mountain bike in a patch of wild roses," she said. "But then, we decided to make a wreath—it was more clean and ethereal looking."

Mel and Chris wrote their own vows, promising always to remain best friends, lovers, partners in adventure, and, most important, mysteries to each other. There was the sense that they saw each other the way climbers view the most difficult, challenging mountains, as full of the unknown, no matter how familiar you may become with them. "I'm absolutely committed to *never* knowing exactly who Chris is," Mel said a few weeks before the wedding. "I don't want to ever get to a point where I think I know what he's thinking. I'm so much more interested in constantly discovering new things about him. I think you make some-one really small when you believe you know them."

Six months after they were married, true to their vision of an adventurous, uncertain life, Mel and Chris quit their jobs in New York, packed up all of their possessions, and moved to Boston, where they had no place to live, no friends or friends of friends to call, and only the vaguest employment plans. "It was Mel and I, shooting from the hip," Chris said. "We didn't know what to expect. But we *like* rocky roads. We are content knowing we don't know what's around the corner."

In Boston, they eventually found jobs—Mel as a lawyer, Chris as a marketing man for a software company. They slowly made friends, discovered places where you can find, in Mel's words, "an awesome burger," and acquired an Aus-tralian sheepdog, which they named Taxi. "We thought it would be funny to go skiing or hiking with the dog in the woods of Vermont and yell, 'Taxi! Taxi!'" Mel explained.

After several months of camping out in a dingy rental, they also found their dream home: an 1870 farmhouse in the countryside outside Boston, with poison ivy growing all over it. The house had been abandoned for years. "Its current res-idents include raccoons, flying squirrels, and thousands of mice," Mel said. "Like everything else Chris and I do, we didn't want a cookie-cutter house. We loved the whole idea that you could live in an environment that was a living, breathing, pain-in-the-ass expression of who you are."

She said that the best part about the house was that it was very scary—partly because of the wildlife living there and partly because they could barely afford the mortgage payments—but they both love to do frightening things. "The house is a huge risk," Mel said. "We bought it for a song, but according to our pocketbooks, it wasn't a song. For us, the house symbolizes that in life if you want to get your dreams to come true, you've got to take action. You've got to step up to the plate and take a swing."

For now, they plan to live in the ramshackle house as is—"We'll be indoor camping for a long time," Mel said— and gradually renovate it by themselves. One of the first things they plan to add to the house is guest bedrooms. Chris and Mel have lots and lots of friends, most of whom they describe as "awesome," and people are always stopping by to visit them. While some couples see their relationship as a private and personal journey, like riding in a sports car with only two seats, Chris and Mel describe theirs as more like a sports utility vehicle, with plenty of room for hiking buddies, sisters and brothers, old roommates from college, childhood soul mates, and long-lost friends who show up in their driveway after a year of traveling around the world or living in a tiny African village.

Most of Chris and Mel's friends are like them—adventurers with little interest in safety, who can talk for hours about surviving in subzero temperatures or how being in love should make you feel as though you're tied to someone else while climbing a slippery glacier—connected, superalert, afraid, and amazed all at once.

When Mel and Chris were married, they gave every guest a booklet, a kind of mini yearbook, filled with pictures and descriptions of their closest friends. It was handmade and heartfelt, with page after page of smiling, tan, not necessarily beautiful but instantly likable people. The descriptions of them were written by Mel and Chris and read like the kind of personal ad you'd definitely answer.

Here are a few descriptions of the kind of people who will fill Mel and Chris's house after the flying squirrels have all been chased out:

Tim Waite: "He and Chris were roommates at the University of Vermont. He is an extremely talented woodworker and currently exhibits his talent designing and building custom-made furniture in Burlington, Vermont. He lives with an excellent woman named Alice, who bakes delicious bread."

D. D. Burlin: "She and Mel were roommates at Dartmouth. She graduated from Georgetown Law and has become an accomplished appellate attorney, river floater, and snowcone maker. She lives in St. Louis with her husband, Johannes, and their two Jack Russell Terriers."

Jeff and Darcy Klausman: "They have been married and living in a cozy log cabin in Idaho for the past two years. Jeff is now finishing his master's in wetland ecology and land restoration at Montana State. He also spends his summers as a fly-fishing guide in Wyoming. Darcy is a practicing nurse, but hot on buying a '73 Ford pickup."

Linda Falzarana: "She is an incredible artist. She also

owns a set design company, Largent Studios, in New York City, and has cool clients like MTV and Red Hot Chili Peppers. On top of her artistic talents, Linda is a snowboarding fanatic and currently lives with her boyfriend, Kevin, in Brooklyn."

As much as Mel and Chris love their friends and their crumbling, unsound, old house, they could leave everything behind at a moment's notice and take off for any far-flung, exotic place. They are not the type of people who get too attached to architecture, chinaware, or the idea of home. "We love it here, but who knows?" Mel said. "If we were to get a call tomorrow and someone said, 'We've got an amazing spot for you over in Thailand, or somewhere that sounded scary and exciting, we'd pack our bags, put the house up for sale, and be out of here in no time."

When I last spoke to Mel and Chris, they had just returned from a fishing trip to Alaska. They had hired a bush pilot to fly them deep into the wilderness and camped there for two weeks, without a phone, a radio, or even a map. Every day they fished for salmon—one of them manned the fishing rod while the other stood on a rock and watched out for grizzlies with a rifle. The salmon, Mel said, weighed forty-five pounds, and when caught on a line, they were so strong they dragged her through the water like a water-skier behind a motorboat.

Mel and Chris travel to places like Alaska partly because it's fun, but mostly the trips are important metaphors for them, reminders of the life they envision together, one filled with a healthy amount of fear and a faster-than-normal heartbeat, with no room for boredom and no hint of security.

"We're *driven* to go on adventures," Mel said. "When we were on this backcountry ski trip in Idaho last winter, the weather was crappy, my pack was heavy, and it was really steep. There were times I was afraid, really afraid I was going to roll right off the mountain. But at the end of the day, I had climbed a mountain on skis, the whole time thinking I couldn't actually make it. That's the way I want to live life, accomplishing things I didn't think were inside me."

When Mel talks, she tends to get on a roll, and she was on a roll now. "I don't think the point in life is to play it safe," she continued. "Chris and I want the kind of life and relationship where we're always up for the next thing. I do not believe the way you win the game is to have a Mercedes in your driveway and the biggest diamond ring of all your friends. I think that's horseshit. There's a great quote by George Bernard Shaw about how he really wanted to feel 'used up' when he died. That's what our life is about, at least the way Chris and I see it. It's about using ourselves up, not just floating along."

A Magnificent

Hunch

SOMETIMES, falling in love is as easy as turning on a switch and going from dark to light, from a person whose answering machine rarely blinks to one whose machine blinks like an SOS signal, with back-to-back messages from a new love.

But sometimes finding love is more like coaxing a cat down from a tree—it takes work, determination, persistence, and a willingness to wait and wait and wait. It can be like a quest with lots of hopeful moments that turn out to be hopeless, like when you spot a parking spot, zoom toward it, and find a fire hydrant. There can be times when you're not at all certain it's love. One of my favorite quotes came from a minister who said, "In a sense, the person we marry is a person about whom we have a magnificent hunch." Even when you walk down the aisle, you can simply be following a hunch, something as ephemeral as a scent of perfume. From interviewing hundreds of brides and grooms, I've come to believe what's most exciting about getting married is not the certainty but the incredible *uncertainty* of love.

Love doesn't have to be like the movies, with fireworks, goose bumps, and soaring background music. It can be so much quieter. You can simply sense a possibility, the way you sense someone strange might be in your house late at night, or that your telephone is about to ring, or that your car is about to break down, or that rain is coming even when it's still sunny.

Holly Lynton, twenty-five, is one of the most determined, willful women I've ever met, the sort of person who once got the recipe for chocolate cake at her favorite restaurant by asking the chef over and over and over again. In fact, some of Holly's friends call her the "small persistent redhead." She is a petite woman with hair as scarlet orange as a tropical sunset, and she never gives up on anything. If she wants an apartment, she will call the landlord a hundred times a day; she will sit in his office all day if necessary, just to convince him to give her the lease. She works as a freelance food and still-life photographer, and if she wants an assignment, she will carry her portfolio, which is almost as large as she is, miles across town, like an ant with a slice of bread, to show her work to an art director or magazine editor. Some people get what they need through luck or beauty, through money or family connections. When it comes to getting what she needs, Holly keeps trying and trying longer than others, and she takes her own zany, inventive, quirky routes.

While growing up in Boulder, Colorado, and New York City, she idolized and imitated her eccentric grandmother, who Holly says was like the city of Venice—mysterious, exotic, complicated, and one of a kind. "She would throw these huge dinner parties and she would do things like have a party with only hors d'oeuvres and desserts because she figured no one really liked the entrees anyway," Holly said. "Or she'd have a chocolate party and make eight chocolate dishes. She was very loving and generous and also extremely difficult. I think I'm a lot like her."

Like her grandmother, Holly rarely does anything in the standard way. She never uses ordinary stationery but instead writes letters on homemade paper, cocktail napkins, Venetian stationery, or the back of her paintings and photographs. Wearing her cameras like bulky necklaces, she has traveled all over the world, often alone with a small backpack full of clothes, film, and watercolors. From a young age, she always felt too idiosyncratic, independent, and terrified of divorce to get married.

She crossed paths with David Poole on April 17, 1992, while they were both standing on a dock on the island of Paros, Greece, waiting for midnight ferries. At the time, he was traveling around Europe with a backpack and an Interail pass, getting by on a shoestring budget, staying in hostels, and taking off for another city or country whenever he pleased. "I was in a Jack Kerouac phase," said David, who is twenty-six and looks exactly like the actor Matthew Modine. "I was on the road, feeling free, chatting up girls on trains. For the past few years, I'd been traveling a lot. I'd been living a country-a-day life, meeting lots of people and never seeing them again. It was like, You're going that way, I'm going this way, no problem."

David grew up on a farm outside London and spent his youth at Haberdashers Askés School for Boys, wearing a uniform and learning how to trade stocks but returning home at night to read adventure and travel novels—ever since he was a young boy, books like Redmond O'Hanlon's *In the Heart of the Congo* and Jack Kerouac's *On the Road* covered his bedside table. He was obsessed with journeys and traveling, and whenever he could, he'd cast off his school uniform and hit the road by himself.

"I'm always going immense distances to casually drop by and visit someone," he said. "I once dropped by to visit my aunt on an island near Tasmania. I like acting as if the world is a small place."

After he graduated from high school, he took a year off to travel around the world by himself. His address book from that period is full of strangers he met on the street in Nairobi or in a nightclub in Amsterdam or on mountain trails in New Zealand. He loved the bumper car–like way he met people, crossing paths for a moment, then turning around and heading off in another direction the next day.

"The whole year was just random meetings with people of all ages and kinds," he said. "I had an around-the-world ticket, so I could just fly off to the next place at will. It was really liberating; there was no sense of commitments; it was nice to just pick up people at random, go into a café, and strike up a conversation, and maybe travel with that person for a month or a week."

Over the years, he had met hundreds and hundreds of people. But he'd never felt an urgency to see them again, a strong hint he should follow—a *magnificent hunch*—until he encountered Holly on the dock.

For Holly, traveling was a more cerebral experience than it was for David. While she also traveled with a backpack and a low budget, she did it in the spirit of someone out of a Henry James novel—to learn, to educate herself, to return from wild experiences abroad more civilized, or at least more interesting at a dinner party. When she met David, she had taken a semester off from Yale University and was spending several months on the Greek island of Paros to study painting at a small art school. It was off season, so she was living in a hotel filled only with students and spent most of her time with a fellow artist, taking photographs and painting watercolor landscapes at an easel set up on a rocky cliff or propped in the middle of a field like a scarecrow. When she met David on the ferry dock, she was on her way to Athens to buy a mountain bike to ride on Paros's bumpy, unpaved roads, which were as curvy as the path of a person dodging a bullet.

David was on his way to Turkey, for no particular reason, just hopping around. "I had been on Paros alone for five days, so I was feeling very mellow and relaxed and also incredibly lonely," he said. "On the dock, I saw this big, pretty blond girl, and she looked sort of chatty so I went over and started a conversation. But she soon lost interest in me so I started talking with this short redhead, no makeup, her hair tied back, wearing a blue Patagonia jacket—that was Holly. We started talking about art, and it was one of those conversations where you find out you're passionate about the same things in about twenty minutes. The fact that we both knew our ferries were about to leave meant we had a fast, intense conversation, and we both realized we wanted to carry on this conversation, despite the poor luck that we were going in opposite directions."

Standing on the dark dock, David remembers, he was struck by the fact that Holly was so petite yet so intense. "She came across as very independent and very confident and very smart," he says. "And organized. She whipped out her Filofax, and no one has Filofaxes when they're budget traveling. She had her backpack and her Patagonia and then this Filofax."

Although Holly could hardly even see David in the darkness, she also felt a magnificent hunch about him, an undertowlike pull in his direction. It wasn't that she fell in love right then, she says, or had any inkling they might end up spending their lives together. But in the half hour they stood on the dock together, she did sense he was a kindred spirit, a guy who would laugh at her jokes, choose the same movies to rent, sit in cafés drinking wine, eating feta cheese, and drawing watercolors on napkins like she does. She sensed the possibility of love in the subtlest way, the way you sense someone watching you from across a restaurant or following you down the sidewalk.

Never one to hesitate, Holly wrote down his address— actually his parents' address in Paris since David didn't have a permanent home at the time. As she wrote it down in her Filofax, she hoped David's name and address wouldn't fade into oblivion over time and become a name she didn't recognize anymore, forlorn as a lost sock. "There was a real sense of urgency about our meeting," she remembers. "It seemed necessary that we somehow manage to hook up again."

Then the ferries arrived blowing their foghorns, and the two went off in opposite directions.

It took Holly, the small persistent redhead, six months to find him again. After she finished art school in Greece, she traveled to Paris and called his parents. David was nowhere near home. By then, he had taken off on another trip, backpacking through Asia. That fall, back at Yale, Holly received a postcard from him, a three-month-old message that had been forwarded from Greece. The postcard said, "Sorry I missed you in Paris. I'll be at the University of California at Berkeley in the fall." Even though David is a wanderer, he always knows where he'll be in a year.

Holly then phoned his parents in Paris again and found out he had left for college and was studying literature. She mailed him a letter at Berkeley, on marbleized Venetian stationery, but it got lost inside a magazine belonging to one of his roommates. It was weeks before he even found it. He stumbled across it in their messy apartment one day, as surprising as a message in a bottle. Over Christmas vacation, he wrote her a postcard from Guatemala, a vague, unemotional note that was all about the colors in the Central American landscape. There was no suggestion that they get together, no warmth in his words, no reference to the dock where they'd met.

It was the most impersonal postcard she'd ever received, but she didn't give up trying to see him again. By now, she couldn't remember much about what he looked like, but she perfectly remembered the feeling she had that night on the dock and, like someone following the scent of great espresso on a back street in Italy, she pursued it. One March night sitting in her apartment, eleven months after they had met, she phoned him.

"I'm a romantic, and I had the idea there was only one person out there for me," she said. "I didn't want to let it go and have that feeling, 'Oh, maybe I should have followed up on that one.'"

Like people who remember exactly where they were when Kennedy was assassinated or when man landed on the moon, David perfectly remembers what he was doing when Holly called. "I was in the shower in my bachelor apartment when the phone rang," he said. "The place was very Zen and practically unfurnished; I had been used to traveling with everything in a tiny backpack. So I jumped out of the shower and answered—I guess I was kind of lonely because a phone call seemed like an important thing.

And it was Holly. I stood there dripping wet, talking on the phone, and I was totally taken by this small persistent redhead. That was the beginning of our phone relationship. She was chatty, flirty, giggly. And she laughed at all my jokes."

After that, they started talking on the phone almost every night, she in her apartment filled with photographs and paintings and he in his spare studio on his bed—the only piece of furniture. "I would call her at two in the morning just as she was going to sleep and tell her bedtime stories," he remembers. "I liked who I was on the phone with her—positive, upbeat, funny."

After two weeks of talking on the phone, she made plans to visit him over spring break. He wasn't exactly prepared for a houseguest. "I had one cup, one spoon, one plate, a backpack, and a Discman plugged into a yard sale hi-fi," he said. "Everything was on the floor. I loved living like I was traveling. I didn't want any stuff or responsibilities. I wanted to be able to take everything I owned on my back. Otherwise, it wasn't worth it."

A week before Holly was supposed to visit, she called David to tell him she'd changed her travel plans—she was going skiing in Aspen instead. "He said, 'Oh, if you change your mind again, just show up,'" Holly remembers. "'If I'm not home, wait for me.' It was so bizarre. I thought, 'Who makes plans this way?' It was so open-ended and unorganized. But I sent him a package over spring break and we kept talking on the phone."

Finally, in May, she did fly out to Berkeley to visit him,

an experience both describe as the most nerve-racking of their lives. When he went to the airport to pick her up, he couldn't picture what she looked like at all. By then, all he could recall from their meeting was a dock at midnight and an interesting girl who kept an organized Filofax.

"I didn't remember anything about her looks except that I had to stoop down to speak to her because she was so small," he said.

When Holly got off the plane, she was so uneasy about meeting this semi-stranger that she wanted to turn around and catch the next flight back to New York. "It was bizarre," she said. "We'd developed this close relationship on the phone, but we had no physical presence to match it with. My plane got in early and he wasn't there, so I walked around the airport and that's where we found each other. He looked different from what I'd imagined. He'd grown his hair, and his nose was bigger than I remembered, and his eyes were sunk back. I thought he was really funny looking."

David's impression of Holly was totally different—he says he fell in love watching her walk toward him with her bags. "When I saw her in the airport, I thought, This is the girl I was talking to? Oh my God!" David remembered. "She had a big smile, her hair glowed orange, she was wearing a yellow dress and tan, suede, high-heeled mules, and she had very clear white skin with freckles. I couldn't believe how beautiful she was."

Later, he gave her a short, one-minute tour of his nearly empty apartment. Like Holly and her grandmother, David rarely does things in a conventional way. For instance, in

Berkeley, he had a habit of entering his apartment through the window, which he always kept unlocked. He just sort of dove into the place, as if he were plunging into a pool. While Holly was visiting, he always opened the window for her to climb in and out of first. In his own way, she thought, he was a perfect gentleman.

The first night Holly was in town, they went out to dinner, and later climbed back through the window into David's apartment. "I was jet-lagged, so he gave me a foot massage, which was pretty strange since he was virtually a stranger," Holly remembered. "There was nowhere in the apartment to sit. There were just these two mattresses. But it felt oddly comfortable. I think we even talked about children, and he said he didn't want to have kids until he was fifty and I said, "Well you're not having them with me, then."

His reply to that was swift. "I quickly came down to thirty," he remembers.

That night, they slept side by side on their mattresses, like two people floating together on the ocean.

After Holly's visit, they began a multicontinental, traveling courtship, getting together in all kinds of different climates and time zones, usually meeting in an airport or train station with their backpacks. They met for a day in Paris the summer after her visit to Berkeley, when both happened to be traveling through the same town at the same time. Then, in March 1994, they spent two weeks together in a seaside town in Portugal, in a small stone house with no heat. "We would go for long walks during the day, and then it would get dark and cold so we'd get into bed and talk all night," David recalls.

In that way, while staying in strange rooms all over the world, for a night or a week at a time, sharing uncomfortable beds and bottles of local wine, they got to know one another. Sometimes a traveling courtship is not a pretty thing—they saw each other with unwashed hair and jet lag and shared many terrible cups of coffee at dawn on smelly trains. But for them, it was as romantic as the adventure novels David used to read as a young boy, full of meetings on foreign street corners and kisses in airports while jets took off overhead.

Traveling together also taught them how to live together. "When you're traveling with someone, you have to work hard and compromise. I might decide I want to go to a museum, while he wants to go on a wilderness hike. David likes to speed through countries, and I like to travel slowly and methodically. We learned to respect each other's rhythms, and we practice that in our daily home life."

In the summer of 1996, David proposed on the island of Paros, where they had first met, while they were staying in a small whitewashed house with cobalt blue window shutters. "We were outside on the terrace eating our Greek salads when he said, 'I wrote a poem and I want your response,'" Holly recalls. "So I'm sitting there soaking up the last piece of feta cheese with bread while he read the poem, which is basically four pages of reasons why I should marry him."

LOVE LESSONS

In many ways, the poem was about David's journey from a wanderer, a guy who lightheartedly traveled from city to city and relationship to relationship, to someone so in love he gets homesick when Holly is in another room.

The poem began with a description of the "old" David:

I wait till I'm prompted to take out the trash
I make love the same way as withdrawing cash
I live for my records, resent any work
Typical jerk

It ended:

Holly Lynton, will you marry me?
Make me the happiest man alive
Say yes and I'll learn to drive
I'll take the trash in
I'll make love with passion
I'll put away childish things
See what bouquets this Casanova brings
We'll have beautiful children
Not repeat out parents' mistakes
For Holly and David junior
I'll do whatever it takes

I love you, Holly, with my mind, body, and soul
I will never stop loving you
Snuggling with you is an out-of-body experience,
Knowing you're sleeping beside me

I know my heart is close by
Watching a movie without you
Is like looking through only one eye
Connections with you are life's greatest highs
Your body is a treasure trove of tingles, giggles, and sighs

Like Holly and David, their wedding was idiosyncratic and out of the ordinary, and it required lots of traveling. They decided to get married in the tiny village of La Peyratte in the Loire Valley of France, at his family's medieval stone house, which is named Le Logis de Thoiré.

While Holly and David are twenty-something, avid travelers who love to throw on a backpack and travel halfway around the world on a moment's notice, both felt entirely ready for marriage. They really wanted to settle down for good—not in one place necessarily, but in one relationship. "I had a real need to say my vows on a natural piece of land," Holly said. "The ground doesn't change, and I wanted to start our marriage on something solid, something that wouldn't fall down years from now or get knocked over or crumble. Both of us come from failed marriages and strange family relationships, and we crave having a firm, stable relationship. I think that's a trend in our generation—we want long commitments."

Le Logis de Thoiré is on a remote winding road and is so old, there are slits in the turrets for shooting arrows at attackers. In a way, the wedding was a perfect metaphor for Holly and David—like their relationship, it required lots of persistence and adventure travel on everyone's part.

Holly and David somehow found a way to persuade a local chef to cook dinner, street musicians to provide the music, and a cranky, reclusive local count to rent them his medieval carriage house as lodging for some of their guests. Their American friends had to fly across the ocean, catch a bus, then find their way to the wedding in a tiny French village populated predominantly by farmers.

"The moral of our story is that all it takes is determination and willpower, regardless of distances, different cultures, time lines, moving around and forwarding addresses, changed phone numbers, money," David said. "All you need to make love work is two people with willpower."

Timing Is

Everything

TIMING IS IMPORTANT to almost every-thing—classical music, the changing seasons, waltzing, surfing, making a soufflé, making a baby. If you plant toma-toes at the wrong time of year, they won't grow. If birds start flying south too early, even a few weeks ahead of schedule, they become disoriented and lose their direction. The same thing happens if people fall in love at the wrong time. Love, like tomatoes and birds, is much more delicate than you might think. If the atmosphere isn't just right, if one person is ready and the other is reticent, then falling in love quickly becomes more like an awkward dance with someone who steps on your toes and makes you feel twenty pounds heavier than you actually are, rather than feather-light. People fall in love at the wrong time all the time—when they're too young, too busy, already married, brokenhearted, not paying attention, or simply not in the mood.

Linda Lopez and Andre Peters have fallen in love several times when the timing was never right. They grew up together in the 1950s, in the Washington Heights neighborhood of New York City, just north of Harlem. "It was before the 1960s riots," Linda remembers. "There were no drugs. You spent your life outside with your peers and came home to sleep and eat and do your homework. I loved all the color and action and noise and people on the street. You don't have that in nonethnic neighborhoods, but you go into an Italian or Hispanic or black neighborhood and there's all that noise."

As a child, Linda spent all of her time outside, where she sought out corners and alleys, places where she wouldn't be noticed, where she was more likely to find old newspapers or alley cats than people. She thought of herself as a wallflower, an ugly duckling. She had bad skin, a serious overbite, a closetful of tight clothes, and a constant sense that she was walking pigeon-toed. Her main memory from that time is feeling uncomfortable, as if she were always dressed for church. "I was overweight," she said. "I can remember walking close to buildings so I wouldn't be noticed. I remember feeling *so* awkward."

Around that time, she fell madly in love with someone who was her total opposite, a tall, athletic, graceful, popular boy named Andre. "He was another neighborhood kid, but a lot older than me," she said. "We were never introduced—I spotted him out on the court playing basketball.

He was a phenomenal player and really cute and five years older than me. It was a killer combination. I mean, forget about it. I was absolutely crazy about him."

For years, he didn't notice her, didn't know she existed, even though she spent almost every Saturday afternoon about ten feet away from him. She'd sit on the fence surrounding the basketball court and watch him play. She'd hang out in the neighborhood candy store, hoping he would stop in for a cherry Coke. Over the years, as she followed Andre around the neighborhood, Linda's looks gradually changed. She transformed from an unpopular, chubby girl into a striking, tall, thin teenager with light brown skin and blue eyes and wild curly hair, a neighborhood beauty. Everyone began noticing her, including Andre. "Linda was gorgeous and beautiful," he remembers. "She had long hair and a fabulous body, and she was quiet and reserved. She came from a strict family. There was a feeling about her that has never left me to this day."

By the time she turned fourteen, they were going steady. When she was a senior in high school, he joined the Air Force and they started writing long love letters to each other every day. "We talked about marriage when I was seventeen," she said. "It was far too young, but people did that then. We were supposed to get married once when he came home on leave. But things just started falling apart. It was clear he wasn't ready."

When asked why he wasn't ready at that time, Andre said, "Adventure, strictly. I was a star athlete. I played basketball for the Air Force. I was in the special forces. I felt I had to have a lot of women. It was just a young boy's greedy attitude about life. I wanted it all, and I did get it all."

When they broke up that time, she burned all of his love letters. "I dumped them in the tub and put some lighter fluid on them and set 'em up," she said.

He saved hers and still has them. "In her letters, she was always waiting for me," he said. "When I read them now, it's very sad. She said, 'I want you and I'm waiting for you.' She could have become very bitter about me, but she didn't. I basically went off and never looked back."

For the next several years, they were out of touch. It was the late sixties, and Linda got an apartment in Brooklyn and started a leather-crafting business making belts and bags. "I was a Woodstock child," she said. "I spent my early twenties at political rallies, going to concerts, taking life-enhancing courses, sitting around philosophizing with my friends. The economy was such that you didn't need a lot to live on. My apartment was between a hundred twenty-five and a hundred fifty dollars a month. There wasn't the pressure to have gainful employment all the time."

Then, in 1970, when Linda was twenty-four, Andre and a friend knocked on her door out of the blue. When she saw him, it was like she was suddenly ten again, admiring him on the playground. "Here he was, a guy out of my past," she said. "My life was so different and I was so different, and yet I still had such strong feelings for him."

They fell back in love and even talked about getting married, but once again the timing wasn't right. While the old spark was there, they had turned into completely different people—he had signed on for a second tour with the Air Force and had fought in Vietnam, while she had become an artsy hippie who spent her weekends marching and protesting against the war. "He was not aware of world affairs, community issues, self-improvement, things that were very important to me at the time," Linda said. "We were so different. He was living day-to-day and having a good time, and I was a lot more serious and intense and probably a lot more unbearable. I think I found him frivolous."

It wasn't long before they parted ways again, but this time Linda was pregnant with their child. "Part of me wanted things to work out, but I started getting signals that Andre wasn't going to do right by me," Linda said. "He started acting really flaky; he still had a lot of wild oats to sow. I thought, Do I saddle myself with a relationship that's going to cause me a lot of grief and tears, or do I get out of it and try to make it on my own? I felt responsible for the baby I was carrying, and I wanted to be happy. Finally, I said, 'I give up. I'm not going to make myself nuts.' It was really terrifying, though. I was barefoot and pregnant, literally."

Soon after leaving Andre, Linda met a man with whom the timing could not have been more perfect. "I was coming back from my mother's at Thanksgiving," she remembers. "I'm pregnant, on the subway, and this guy walks over to me. He's eating an ice cream cone, and he stops in front of me and says, 'Would you like some?' I thought, 'Oh my

God, what a jerk!' But somehow we got to talking, and by the time we reached Flatbush, we'd made a date. That guy and I spent the next six years together. He moved in with me, he took care of me, he was there when my child was born, he was there through good times and bad. He was a gift, such a gift to me."

Linda named her daughter Jennifer, though Andre didn't learn that for years. As far as Linda was concerned, he had disappeared off the face of the earth, even though he eventually moved into an apartment in her neighborhood. Over the years, he ran a community center on the Upper West Side, then he opened a bar and restaurant in Harlem called The Salt and Pepper. He stayed single, and whenever he wanted to, he took off traveling around the world. "I'd go here or there for a month," he said. "I spent time in the islands. I was doing whatever I really wanted to do. I was the type of person who would just get in my car and drive to California without saying a word, and no one would know where I went. I did things at will and at whim. I was a rogue."

At one point, he decided it was time to get married and he did, but it lasted about as long as one of his cross-country drives. "We were best friends," he said. "But it wasn't a love affair. After that, I was alone for a long time."

During those years, Linda closed her leather-making business and began taking voice and acting lessons. Her subway romance ended. She got a disc jockey's license and struggled as a single mom. Eventually, she was hired to work as a deejay at a rock 'n' roll station in Poughkeepsie, New York.

"I took Jenny out of school and we moved up there, lock, stock, and barrel," Linda remembers. "It's always exciting when you follow your heart, but it was very difficult. I worked the graveyard shift, midnight to six. We were living in a two-family house so there was someone around to watch Jenny all the time, but I would put her to bed at nine, slip out at eleven-thirty, come home, get her up and ready for school, sleep while she was in school, then pick her up. It was grueling."

For Jennifer, being the only child of a hardworking single parent was never as sad or as lonesome as some people might imagine. "I think I'm atypical," said Jennifer. "My life was very complete with my mother just being the one parent. I was happy. But my mother is very strong. She's the sort of person who picks up the slack and covers all the bases."

In many ways, Jennifer is like her mother. She has the same wild hair and the same raspy friendly voice, along with a womanly strength that comes across even over the telephone. They are both survivors who have been through plenty of unhappiness and ended up funnier, friendlier, and kinder because of it, the way blue jeans end up softer if you wash them with rocks. They are also busy women who talk, walk, and make decisions quickly. They don't read the menu over and over in restaurants, unable to decide what to order. Instead, they open the menu, decide, close it. One imagines they wouldn't spend much time choosing anything from a house to a wedding dress.

Even Jennifer's love life has been very similar to her mother's, shaped by good timing and bad. Like her mother, Jennifer fell madly in love when she was very young, still a teenager, and became pregnant. But the father of her child wasn't ready to settle down yet, and he ended up breaking Jennifer's heart so badly she described it as a multiple fracture. Around that time, while she was still reeling from the breakup and feeling panicky about being a new mom, she was introduced to Kevin Krieger. She wasn't ready for a new love at all; actually, she was thinking she might try to avoid men for the rest of her life. It seemed to her that falling in love was like riding a bicycle in deep snow—good balance was impossible and some kind of injury inevitable.

But Kevin was ready for love and willing to wait it out and wait it out, until the timing was right for her. "Kevin fell in love with me right away, but I had all this stuff going on with the other guy coming in and out of my life," Jennifer said. "So we were friends, good, good, good friends for about six months and then, as I healed from my first relationship, I opened my eyes and he was there and I fell in love with him."

She added, "You really do have to be in a certain place to receive what's out there for you."

By the time Jennifer was twenty-three, she was a full-time mom with three children, living with Kevin in Chicago. Two of the children, the girls, have their mother's and their grandmother's crazy hair, full of ringlets, cork-screws, and electricity—the kind of hair that makes you think they would enjoy roller coasters.

Like Linda, Jennifer is an earthy, warm, natural lioness of a mother. She says she fell in love with her children the moment they were born, something that seems utterly impossible and foreign to me. When my son was born, I felt total fear. I remember thinking I'd made the biggest, most long-lasting mistake of my life—you can get out of almost everything, even a marriage contract. But you can't get out of motherhood.

Luckily, time changes everything. Now, almost four years later, I'm so crazy about my son I can watch him sleep for hours, with total fascination. I think his toes are more beautiful than the coast of Ireland.

While Jennifer loved her children easily and instantly, motherhood had an unexpected side effect: She began to miss her father for the first time in her life. She and Linda had only seen him twice over the years, once when Jennifer was five and again when she was thirteen. Other than that they hadn't spoken to Andre in more than twenty years.

"I felt I needed to touch base with him," Jennifer said. "I wanted to let him know he had grandkids, fill him in. I told my mother, and she said, 'If you want to catch up with him, I'll give you the number of a girlfriend of mine, Rosemary, who might cross paths with him every now and then.' So, I called Rosemary, and she said he was still in Washington Heights. She hadn't seen him but I could leave my number at a restaurant where he hangs out. So she went to the restaurant with a note that said, 'Jenny wants to talk to you.'"

The restaurant where Rosemary left the note was called the Gold Brick Inn, Andre's favorite hangout. He walked in one afternoon and found the note waiting there for him, as surreal and surprising as being paged in an airport in a city where you don't know anybody. "I thought something was terribly wrong so I immediately called Jennifer," Andre remembers. "The phone call was a little eerie. I felt love for my daughter and then I felt what had been missing from my life. I thought, Wow, this is what I needed all the time."

Jennifer remembers that their conversation was both easy and uneasy. "It was awkward but it was a relief," she said. "I didn't know if he was alive or dead. That was my number one question. Is he around? Did I wait too long?"

To Jennifer's surprise, she and her father started talking on the phone almost every day and became real buddies. A few months after she left the note for him, Jennifer and her children traveled to New York City. She asked her mother *and* her father to pick her up at the airport. When she walked off the plane, Linda and Andre were standing there together. "It was weird, it was surreal, it was Mom and Dad," Jennifer remembered.

It was even stranger for Linda, who called the whole situation "a heart-pounder." As she remembers, "There was no great dramatic scene or anything. We didn't talk a lot, it was just sort of quiet, and really weird."

For Andre, the airport reunion wasn't weird or uncomfortable at all. It was as if nothing had changed, as if time hadn't passed. "I always feel the same way when I see Linda," he said. "The first thing I think about is how much I love her. That feeling never left. It was always there. When love is genuine, I don't think you can escape it no matter what you do."

In the movies, if an absent father was meeting his long-lost daughter at the airport, the father would probably be nervous and shuffling his feet and feeling tremendously guilty. Andre was simply happy. "When I saw Jennifer at the airport, it was hugs and kisses and *'Come here!'*" he remembered. "It was very easy to fall back into it. I realized she was my baby. We look exactly alike."

For Andre, meeting Jennifer and Linda at the airport felt like the end of a journey, he said, the end of his wanderings, his wanderlust, his wild, solo adventures. "It was such a nice feeling," he remembers. "For the first time, I had a sense of family responsibility, of love, of bringing things together. It was a real family, grandkids and all. It was like I was being introduced to what life is really all about."

That night, Andre gave Linda a ride home. They drove in silence, she remembers, but after that, they started talking on the phone occasionally. Then, as she put it, they began "sort of getting together again." This time, Andre was ready, even anxious, to fall in love and settle down—but Linda wasn't. "I was actually seeing someone else at the time, a pretty serious relationship, so I was just friends with Andre for a year and a half," Linda said. "He knew about this other guy, and I guess he was just waiting for his opportunity. Eventually, he got it.

The other relationship didn't work out, and I ended up crying on Andre's shoulder about it."

Finally, almost forty years after Linda first spotted Andre on the basketball court and started trailing him through the neighborhood, they were both ready for love at the same time, ready to share closet space, morning coffee, cross-country drives, and grandparenting. Some things hadn't changed at all—though Andre's hair was now the dark gray shade of thunderclouds, he still played basketball, and Linda still loved to watch him.

In some ways, remeeting an old love is like opening a jewelry safe on a sunken ship after many years under water, and looking for a diamond ring you know was once there. When you open the safe, you don't know if the diamond will still be intact, if it will be ruined, corroded, stolen, washed away, or lost. For Linda and Andre, love was still there with its old strong sparkle. In some ways, love like that is all the more amazing for having been buried and survived. "If I know my mother, I have a feeling she loved my father all along," said Jennifer. "I think love was always there, but she stored it away."

That's the thing about love—sometimes, it has the endurance of the "black box" on an airplane, something that is built to survive plane crashes and keeps emitting signals so it can be found anywhere, in snowdrifts, deep forests, swamps. Many people believe you can never go home again and you can also never go back to old loves, especially not loves from childhood. But I like to think you sometimes can, that there are certain loves, and home-towns, worth returning to.

For Linda and Andre, their romance started up again slowly, at the pace of a Sunday afternoon walk in balmy weather. It was easy and unstrained, but not instantaneous. "In the beginning we spent a lot of time reminiscing, catching up with each other and talking about what we had done over the years and what became of old friends," Linda remembers. "He had done what many men do, sown his wild oats and calmed down. A permanent relationship and continuity had become more important to him than going from girl to girl."

Jennifer, who had never seen her mother and father in the same room, let alone holding hands, was amazed to watch them becoming girlfriend and boyfriend. To this day, she swears she wasn't acting as a matchmaker when she asked them both to meet her at the airport. "It wasn't my intention or even my expectation that they would get back together," Jennifer said. "It was a total surprise. They started spending more and more time together. Then, I used to call my dad and my mom would be there, or I'd call my mom and my dad would be there. That was kind of a clue."

As Jennifer sees it, their reunion wasn't like an old-fashioned fairy tale where love happens with a single bolt of lightning or a wave of a magic wand—it was more like a *modern* fairy tale—complicated, difficult at times, painful as well as perfect.

"They had a lot of talking and catching up to do, a lot of healing and questions and answers," Jennifer said. "They started off slow, but you could see the feelings were there. You could see that they were happy and light together. And he is so good to me and his grandchildren. He's so right for all of us. You wonder how so much time could have passed."

Just as Linda is not the type of person to fret over a menu, she doesn't dwell on the question of why it took so long for things to work with Andre. She only occasionally wishes they'd managed to stay together when they were young, so they could have bought their first dinner plates and car together, had more children, and appeared in each other's photographs over the years. Still, Linda says, it's almost as if Andre *was* in all the photos she took, as if he were sitting across from her at all the dinner tables in all her different apartments, that he was never gone completely. "I am surprised sometimes when I look at Andre and think about how long we've known each other and how much of our lives we've been connected," Linda said. "It started so long ago. And even though we were living separate lives, there was always that connection. It's surprising and profound and very emotional. I think some people just match."

The moral of their story, she says, is simple: Follow your heart even if it leads you away from love for the time being.

"The lesson I got out of this was: do the right thing," Linda said in her earthy, gravelly voice. "I think the decision I made when I was twenty-four, to be on my own, was really smart. I thought about what would be good for my soul, and at the time, even though it meant not being with the man I loved, I was true to myself. And it worked out. I often think if we'd stayed together then and the timing wasn't right and we tried to force the situation and didn't listen to our hearts, we would have ended up in divorce court, hating each other. When we came back together, we were complete people who had been true to ourselves."

Unlike Linda, Andre spends entire days dwelling on the past. "I regret the years apart," he said. "I get very hurt about that. I just took the wrong path. But now, it's been corrected. This time, the timing was great. We're still very healthy and the love is still there."

On September 21, 1996, they were married on a bluff in Washington Heights, their old neighborhood, overlooking the Hudson River. "It was the most beautiful day of the year," Linda said. "I did all this weather research, and we came up with the one day when it never seemed to rain, and sure enough it was a sunny, beautiful, eighty-degree day. We had quite a few friends there from when we were kids, and everybody kept saying, 'It's about time.' All along, everybody thought, 'What's taking them so long, what's wrong with them?' Everybody seemed to see it except us."

Their granddaughters were the flower girls, their grandson was the ringbearer, and Jennifer cried nonstop. "It was truly romantic," Jennifer said. "They were so young when this story began, and it was really an incomplete story, especially the way they went their separate ways without any real resolution. The way the story ends, it's really a finish. They've completed the circle. It's what everybody wishes they could do, to go back and have another chance and make something work."

Love at First

Sight

DURING THE YEARS I've spent on the "love beat," my view of romance has changed a lot. Before I started this job, I did not believe in love at first sight. I thought that instant chemistry, eyes across a crowded room, lightning bolts, and hearts that pounded like the soundtrack to *Jaws* were experiences people made up to prove their love was real. To me, instant love was like UFOs, a phenomenon people wanted to believe in because it seemed so magical and mysterious, it connected them to the heavens, and it made being human so much more exciting. I rolled my eyes when friends described falling in love on the spot, just as I roll my eyes when people return from vacations saying the sky was cloudless the whole time and they got bumped up to first class "just because" and movie stars were staying in their hotel. Sure! Fat chance! I know you were riding in crummy old coach just like the rest of us. Admit it: Vacations and love are never *that* amazing.

But by now, I've heard so many stories about love at first sight that I do believe in it. I think you really can spot true love in another person's eyes, like seeing a fish flash its tail under the surface of dark water. You can know a person is right for you even before you know his name. The experience, I've been told many times, is a lot like being bumped up into first class just as you're boarding a plane—within moments, you're elevated to a place where people offer you champagne, turbulence doesn't seem as scary, *life* doesn't seem as scary, and everyone is smiling. You feel unbelievably lucky.

Once I interviewed a classical actor named Peter Francis James who fell instantly in love with an underwater archeologist, Jillian Nelson. She is tall and lithe and has long, wavy blond hair, and more than once she's been asked by children if she was a mermaid. Her nickname is Splash. Peter fell madly in love with her the moment he saw her, years ago, working behind a cash register at a restaurant called Le Peep in Minneapolis.

"I asked her for change for cigarettes," he remembers. "I asked her what time they open and what time they close. I asked every civilized question I could ask other than 'Who are you and will you be my wife?'"

When I was in my early twenties, I lived with a few friends in California, in a small white house with blue window shutters across from a golf course. We were all struggling writers who always seemed to have either broken hearts or broken cars or both. But every now and then, we'd walk out of the house and find signs of hope—neon yellow or orange golf balls on the lawn, lying there like Easter eggs or colorful hail. Everyone needs some magic in their lives and at the time, that was ours. Whenever I hear a love-at-first-sight story these days, I think of those golf balls, which I used to save. Sometimes, love just drops into your life like that, a bright, accidental, and magical thing.

That's how it was for Maureen Sherry and Steven Klinsky. He first saw her one rainy night in New York City when he was riding in a cab. She had just broken up with a longtime boyfriend and was walking on the sidewalk, sobbing as openly as if she were at home with the shades pulled down and the answering machine on.

"She's very attractive and she was crying and it was a strange misty evening and I said to the driver, "Stop the cab here," remembers Steven, an investment banker. "I was in a melancholy mood, and seeing this woman walking up the street triggered something in me. So I ran after her and tapped her on the shoulder and introduced myself."

I don't think there's an explanation for why some people recognize their soul mate in a total stranger, especially one who's sobbing and soaking wet from the rain. Some of it may be luck or location or chemistry or even desperation. But whatever the explanation, love at first sight is like a campfire, an almost primordial thing. It's an instinct, an inner version of road maps and highway signs pointing out the right way to go.

My all-time favorite love-at-first-sight story was told to me by Paisley Knudsen and Karl Schade. They fell in love instantly, when she was a junior at Pomona College in southern California and he was a freshman at nearby Claremont College.

Paisley has red curly hair and eyes the light green color of grasshoppers. She is lighthearted about almost everything, including her unusual name. "At least they didn't name me Plaid or Polka Dot," she says.

While some children are brought up to be polite or lawyerly, she was brought up to laugh. "My mother always told me, 'Be cute, responsible, and fun,'" Paisley remembers. "She also said, 'If there's a laugh or cry situation, always try to laugh.' So whenever I fell down as a kid, I had to laugh."

Growing up in San Francisco, Paisley was a fanciful, whimsical child with a closetful of ballgowns, scarves, capes, and patent leather shoes. Ever since she can remember, she has loved dressing up and wearing long gowns with trains that dragged on the sidewalk, in the mud, it didn't matter. Almost all of her ballgowns had puffy sleeves, which she loved because she could store a menagerie of stuffed animals in them. Her favorite piece of furniture was a large velvet mushroom in her bedroom—she would spend hours sitting underneath it in one of her gowns pretending she and her animals were in the forest.

Paisley's parents divorced when she was five, and she lived with her mother, Fritha, a zany, red-haired, impish woman who describes herself as a "sixties hippie mom."

While Paisley was growing up, Fritha worked as a costume designer for the San Francisco opera and drove a lime green convertible Fiat that matched her eyes.

Paisley's wardrobe completely confounded her mother. "I lived in jeans, and here I had this princess who had to have high white socks every day, black Mary Janes, and what she called her 'ballgown'—a plaid dress with puffy sleeves and petticoats," Fritha said. "And a big velvet cape with a big hood. That was her signature piece. She would *not* wear pants. I couldn't believe she was my daughter. It felt like she had dropped in from somewhere else."

Paisley was so particular about her clothes she wore purple velvet knickers in gym class. When deciding what to wear, she said, she always chose clothes that would make her feel as if she had "one foot on earth and another foot in heaven."

Besides ballgowns and velvet capes, she loved forests. She climbed trees, not because she was a tomboy or particularly athletic but because she believed that fairies and other magical wood creatures lived among the branches and she wanted to introduce herself to them. "I used to sit in the trees and write poetry or play the harp," recalls Paisley, who is now a twenty-three-year-old novelist and professional harpist. "I remember one time I ran away from school and disappeared into the woods, wearing a big poufy dress and hoping to be raised by wolves. I thought the forest was where all the magic was."

Her mother recalls, "We used to hike a lot when Paisley was a child, and it would take forever because she would have to say hello to all the imaginary crickets and pick flowers and talk to the fairies."

As a young girl, Paisley was quiet, soft-spoken, and pensive rather than popular. "She was a little reclusive," said her mother. "I always said, 'She's going to live in a little nest in her pajamas and play her harp.'"

Paisley's upbringing was as unconventional as her purple knickers. Fritha used to pick her up from school in the lime green Fiat, often dressed in costumes and wigs she was working on. "She would come in a full anchovy head or an ice queen headpiece," remembers Paisley. "The anchovy was particularly alarming. She had big pop-out eyes and aluminum foil scales. I was too young to be embarrassed, but she did learn to embarrass me over the years."

On nights when Fritha was having parties, she would put Paisley to sleep at five in the afternoon and wake her up at midnight so she wouldn't miss the fun. "There was one particularly amazing party I remember," Paisley said. "It was a costume party, and my mother was a goddess and she had a water slide that went out the back door into the yard. She woke me up at midnight, and it was my first all-nighter. I was seven."

When it came to her own love life, Fritha took an adventurous, come-what-may, live-life-to-the-fullest approach. "My mother is very free in terms of who she dates," Paisley said. "She doesn't care about age. She's gone out with very young men and her oldest was eighty-six."

Growing up, Paisley and Fritha were more like close buddies than mother and daughter. Once Paisley reached her teens, she and her mom even double-dated sometimes. "My mother and I once dated matadors together," Paisley remembers. "Portuguese matadors. That was our bullfight stage."

However, down deep, their views of love were as different as their clothing styles. From an early age, Fritha taught Paisley that love comes and goes as naturally as the tide and it's never a good idea to expect it to stay.

"My mother's favorite quote is, 'I do men in decades,'" Paisley said. "Her feeling is there are lots of matches in the world, and if you fall in love and have ten years together, that's wonderful. If it lasts longer, great. But if it doesn't, there is always someone else. My mother says she doesn't know who she'll marry next. She's got guys lined up, guys saying, 'Oh, I want to be number five.' For me, I'd rather fall in love for life instead of decades."

Unlike her mother, Paisley was a hopeless romantic from very early on. Sitting underneath her mushroom as a child, dressed in her ballgowns and velvet scarves, she dreamt of finding true, old-fashioned, long-lasting, knee-weakening love. "I used to wish for true love whenever I saw a hay bale, a white horse, the first star, or whenever I went over railroad tracks," she said. "I've wished for true love my whole life. True love, that's all I wanted."

Paisley's first e-mail address was TrueLove.

As soon as she arrived at Pomona College as a freshman, Paisley went about decorating her tiny dorm room with her usual sense of whimsy and otherwordliness. "I tried to make my room look like heaven," she said. "I had two harps on opposite sides of the room so it looked like the gates of heaven. My bed looked like a big cloud with all the white featherdown pillows. Everything in my room was white—white towels, white walls, white lights."

Her love life in college, however, was far from heavenly. She had many boyfriends, all somehow the wrong match for her—being with them was like driving in a car seat ergonomically adjusted for someone else. "I dated many people in college," Paisley said. "I met guys, had my heart broken many times, like ripped apart, *shredded*. Finally, I said, 'Forget it.' My girlfriends and I decided to go to parties in a group, power en masse, and just dance. Forget men."

To emphasize her antimen attitude, she cut off all her hair and totally forgot about finding true, old-fashioned love. Instead, she went around scowling at happy-looking couples and shouting things like "Power to Women!" She had completely stopped believing in the possibility of long-lasting or even interesting marriages. "Whenever I thought about marriage, I thought, I'll have to settle," she remembers. "I'll have to find true love in something else, my harp or my children."

Then, one night during Paisley's senior year, she was with her girlfriends at a dance at Claremont College, not a place where she ever enjoyed hanging out. "I'd avoided Claremont for years," she said. "They were the jocks, the business guys, the heartbreakers. We dated the scientists, the biologists, the artists."

Late that night, while hanging out on the edge of the dance floor and thinking how corny all the slow-dancing couples looked, Paisley spotted Karl Schade. He caught her eye the way an automobile speeding toward you from an unexpected direction does. Paisley describes herself as the sort of person who avoids eye contact like some people avoid beestings, but she stared and stared and stared at Karl, and he stared right back.

"He was actually leaving with another woman when he saw me," remembers Paisley. "He dropped her hand and I dropped my friends and we just started dancing together. It was literally like the whole room went fuzzy and dark and it was just us. It was so dark I couldn't even tell what he looked like. I just knew what it felt like to be with him. It felt perfect."

She added, "Neither of us remembers speaking at all, but we were definitely flirting in our dancing. He was not just a great dancer, he was a great partner. Karl was the first man I ever met who danced with me, he engaged me, he played off my moves. He's a nut on the dance floor. We really connected while we were dancing."

Much later that night they left the dance together, still staring at each other, and weaved across campus like students who had been drinking way too many margaritas. Eventually, they ended up back at his dorm room. "College wisdom says don't go to a secluded place on the guy's territory," Paisley said. "But I didn't care. We had so much to talk about. It was like we were almost trying to catch up with each other, like we hadn't seen each other in a long time. It was like, Here's my life, here's who I am. I wanted to go fast-forward."

Sitting on the bed in his dorm room, they talked until daylight. "It was like, I'm fascinated with you. Tell me more," Paisley remembers. "When I finally had to go, he asked for my phone number, and I wanted him to call so badly that I wrote it on both of his hands, on a few pieces of paper, one in his wallet and one in his pocket. He had my phone number *everywhere*. The next day, he called me at three on the dot, which I remember and he remembers. We went to dinner and a movie. He wore a big flannel shirt and jeans. I thought, Wow, he's cute. My girlfriends were all hiding in various places around my dorm so they could see him."

While Karl and Paisley fell in love quicker than a red light changing to green, they are an unlikely pair, opposites in most ways. She speaks in long sentences that are poetic and flowery, like paisley. He, on the other hand, is reserved, conservative, and straightforward as a pin-striped tie. While she grew up in San Francisco, he grew up in a tiny town in Arizona, in a house between a cotton field and a Kmart. He was voted Most Likely to Succeed and Best Dressed in high school. She wore all black in high school (she'd grown out of ballgowns by then) and traveled in a crowd of moody artists. Her friends were not particularly interested in succeeding.

"I only went out with tall, dark, artistic guys, and Karl is this big beefy stud," Paisley says. "He's a jock. He's into finance. He's more normal than anyone I ever went out with. One of my ex-boyfriends is studying and trying to find Bigfoot. Then there was Aaron, who thinks he's an alien. He had pebbles glued to the doors of his car. Aaron had a wonderful heart of gold, but he was a little strange. Karl is an all-American star quarterback who dated the head cheerleader. He was everything I was scared of. We were totally different, but he always had the same sort of hope for true love that I had."

Karl says he was so crazy about Paisley's "mysterious beauty and funky flair" that he sent her about sixty roses the first week they knew each other. "Paisley is everything I am not and wish I could be," he said. "She comes from a very artistic background, she's much more open-minded than I am. I'm basically a better person because of her, and I hope I can return the favor."

After only two weeks, they began talking about eloping to Las Vegas, although both knew they would probably get married in a more traditional way, especially since Paisley had loved ballgowns her entire life.

"Before I met Karl, everyone told me, 'When you fall in love, you'll know. You'll just know,'" Paisley said. "I never believed that. But I finally understand what it means to 'know.' I think there are all these different voices inside you that tell you this isn't right or this doesn't feel good. When I met Karl, all the voices were silenced. Everything was at peace. I wasn't having internal arguments. I wasn't worrying about how I looked. I was just happy all the way through, right down to the core. That's the 'I know' feeling."

When Paisley told her parents she had fallen instantly and madly in love with another student and that they were thinking about getting married, her mother and father had totally different reactions. Her father was mainly worried about how they would support themselves. "My dad was more concerned with my finding someone who would take care of me," she said. "But my mother said, 'Just make sure he takes care of your heart.' She's married for love twice, and she hopes to do it many times more."

Karl and Paisley became formally engaged a few months after they met, during spring break in Mexico. They drove down there with some classmates and spent a week camped out in a friend's backyard, sleeping on rickety lawn chairs under a sky so packed with stars it looked like a dark concert hall dotted with thousands of burning matches and lighters.

"Every night we'd go sit by this palm tree and watch the waves," Paisley remembers. "One night, Karl said, 'When we drive back to California, I want to stop and buy you a diamond ring.' So in San Diego, we stopped at the first jewelry store we could find."

When Karl got back to school and told his friends he'd proposed to Paisley, they all looked at him as if he'd joined a strange cult that required its members to wear purple robes. "All my friends, every single one of them, said, 'Are you crazy?'" Karl recalls. "I actually lost friends because of it. It's not acceptable for men my age to be in favor of marriage and commitment whereas it's very rewarding for women. Men have to almost act like a guy's guy while being committed at the same time."

Six days after his college graduation, Karl became even more committed. He and Paisley, both barely over twenty-one, were married in a private log cabin deep inside one of Paisley's favorite forests—a grove of redwood trees hundreds of years old, in northern California. It was the sort of place Paisley had always wanted to live in as a child. The cabin was not only surrounded by trees, it was furnished with them. In fact, you could climb trees in the main room. Four enormous redwoods grew right through the roof.

Paisley's dress fell to her ankles and was just short enough to reveal her white patent leather high-heeled Mary Janes. It also had an enormous, fanciful train that bubbled like a Jacuzzi as she walked through the forest to the ceremony. "One friend of mine said the train looked like a bunch of giant marshmallows were chasing me," she said. She also wore a paisley cape, like the ones she wore into the woods as a child for a tea party with the fairies.

Paisley's mother wore a leopard print dress and bright red shoes to the wedding. She looked like an exotic tropical bird that had mistakenly landed in a California forest. When asked about matrimony, she said, "I really like marriage! I'm sure I'll do it again."

When Paisley and Karl mailed out the invitations for their wedding, they asked guests to send words of advice back with their replies. "My dad wrote, 'Elope,'" recalls Paisley. "That was his word of advice. Another person wrote, 'Get a prenup.' Everybody thought we were crazy to marry so young. They asked us, 'Why?' But we thought, Why not? We're going to be together anyway. We have no doubts. Karl and I are both very headstrong, and we won't ever give up. We just won't. We'll just push our way through whatever comes."

I visited Paisley recently, halfway through her first year of marriage. She and Karl live in a clean, small apartment filled with sunlight. On the afternoon I spent there, Paisley's red hair looked like a small brushfire, it was so filled with light. She spends her days now working on a novel, and Karl is a junior investment banker. Shyly, she showed me the scrapbook she had begun, documenting their marriage so far. "Here is Karl on his first day of work," she said. "Here is our first dinner party. Eight people on a couch."

She says she thinks her marriage is as strong as a redwood tree. Because they fell in love so quickly, and on such a gut level, she sees her relationship as something almost otherworldly, like a shooting star that fell into her lap. It was all magic, the sort of love she used to dream about while sitting underneath the mushroom in her bedroom. She certainly never had to make a list of pros and cons, or have heart-to-heart talks with her best friends about whether Karl was the right person for her.

She also said married life suited her. A person with a strong nesting instinct, she even loved baking and vacuuming. "I've had the argument with many people about whether marriage changes you or not," she said. "I think it does. When we go on vacation now, we're Mr. and Mrs. rather than two wild lovebirds. People treat you as more of a sacred unit, and I love that."

Couples like Paisley and Karl amaze me, I have to say.

I've been married almost ten years, and I still lie in bed at night sometimes, looking up at the plastic glow-in-the-dark stars we taped on the ceiling a long time ago and wondering whether I made the right decision. At those times, the dishes pile up in our sink, darkening my thoughts further. But then, a day or two later, my husband will make a great joke or his eyes will gleam that fantastic blue I've always loved or he'll read my mind incredibly accurately, and I'll be reassured again. That's how my marriage has lasted, leapfrogging from perfect moment to perfect moment, with fear of falling in between. But some couples, like Paisley and Karl, not only find their love instantly but never seem to question it. They never go through periods where dirty dishes fill their sink. Still, as inspiring and lucky as they are, I try not to envy them too much. I don't think anyone should. I've seen lots of other couples whose relationships were like VW bugs from the sixties, covered with nicks and dents, with thousands and thousands of ragged miles on them, but powering on nonetheless.

As newlyweds, Paisley and Karl have received all kinds of advice on everything from how to save money to how to make love last. "My dad believes marriage is like a rose garden—you have to constantly weed," Paisley said. "He says that when he and my mother were married, the weeds took over the roses. So now he calls me all the time and says, 'Are you weeding the garden?'"

If she's asked, Paisley gives her own advice on love. "When my friends tell me, 'I can't find the one,' I tell them,

'Stop thinking about it, and it will run right into you,'" she said.

On the day I visited her, Paisley seemed madly, effortlessly in love. Like her, the whole apartment glowed. Her harp caught the sun like a mirror, and the living room was filled with pictures, paintings, and sculptures of beaming, beautiful angels. "There's one gargoyle," said Paisley, pointing to an ugly stone creature on a windowsill. "That belongs to Karl. He got it to counteract the angels because they're so girly."

Paisley definitely found the kind of love she always wished on hay bales and white horses for—old-fashioned, instant, thunderbolt love. "I think falling in love with Karl is part of a bigger historical picture for me," Paisley said. "It's part of something my parents started and I'm trying to finish. My parents called themselves the Sunshine Family, but their sunshine went out after a few years. I'm trying to change that and make a family with real sunshine."

Green

Bananas

AT SEVENTY-TWO, Clarice K. Olinger is anything but a stereotypical senior citizen. You would never use the word *elderly* to describe her. Her hair is naturally black and curly, and she drives very, very fast, zooming up her long driveway like a teenager. She is thin and energetic, runs a mile every day, takes aerobics classes, and seems to have none of the usual fears of old age, from indigestion (she loves spicy foods) to loneliness to broken bones to burglars. While some older people stay inside when it snows, peering out the windows like concerned cats, Clarice marches out and shovels. If it snows A LOT, she goes cross-country skiing.

After her first husband died in 1985, Clarice stayed on alone in their big, airy, white house in Basking Ridge, New

Jersey. The house is at the end of a long driveway and surrounded by big trees that creak and moan when the wind
blows, like the soundtrack to a horror movie. It is a house
with old plumbing and heating systems, full of metallic
bangs and loose windowpanes that shake in the wintertime
like teeth chattering. It's the sort of house that would seem
terrifying at Halloween *without* decorations. But Clarice is
never afraid there. She turns off all the lights at night and
sleeps as easily as if her whole family—her ex-husband and
five children, now grown—were still down the hall in their
rooms. "My mother is a great role model," said Barbara
Olinger, one of her daughters, a yoga teacher who lives in
Los Angeles. "She lives life without fear."

After her husband died, Clarice continued to wear her
wedding ring. She didn't feel ready even to think about
falling in love again. In fact, she didn't believe love was possible at her age. Once you were in your sixties or seventies,
she thought, people talked about falling on the ice or
falling down stairs, but never falling in love. Aerobics might
be possible at her age, even hiking in Nepal, but she
thought real romance was as out of the question as bearing
children.

Four years after becoming a widow, though, she did begin to think an evening date might be nice here and there.
So one day she slipped her wedding ring off—for months
afterward there was a pale mark where the ring used to be,
like a tan line left over from a vacation. She announced to
her friends, many wanna-be matchmakers, that she was

"looking for someone." She wasn't looking for a lot, though—the most she hoped to find was a man who might provide pleasant conversation on a Saturday night.

Searching for that, she set out in the winter of 1990 for a singles discussion group held in a church in Morristown, New Jersey. She had read about the event in the newspaper and attended it alone, without knowing anybody. As it turned out, she walked into a room mostly full of singles in their twenties and thirties who were flirting and exchanging business cards. It was as if she were a forty-year-old walking into a high school prom—most people there were a generation or two younger than she.

Clarice is not the sort of person to be intimidated at a party and hover on the edge of the room, out there where the shy and nervous people gather. Clarice is always in the center where conversation flows like the dancing at an old-fashioned ball, with one person cutting in after another after another, never leaving an awkward or quiet moment. It was the same at the singles group. She just jumped in fearlessly, starting one conversation after another until eventually she was introduced to an older gentleman named Victor Lindner.

Victor had never been to a singles event before, but he was looking for love with as much determination as someone looking for his lost wallet. "It was a lonely hearts group," he said. "People come to discuss things, but actually they are looking out of the corner of their eyes for people they might find attractive."

Like Clarice, Victor doesn't seem at all elderly. Now eighty-one, he works full-time as an associate technical director of a military arms research center in Dover, New Jersey. Widowed in 1989, he windsurfs, canoes, hikes, loves to buy clothes in thrift shops, and is fearless about almost everything from wearing stripes with polka dots to sitting in hot tubs others might worry would stop their hearts. When he met Clarice, he had just begun dating again, but with little success.

"My father was a widower, and after a certain period of time, it was clear he wanted to find a friend," said Vicki Lindner, Victor's daughter, who teaches creative writing at the University of Wyoming. "He'd go out with women, but he said it was very depressing. They'd talk about how they couldn't stand their dead ex-husbands, and that made him nervous."

Clarice remembers feeling "an instant zap" when she was introduced to Victor. "Vic is a warm, gregarious person, witty and bright and very well educated," she said. "He has a twinkle in his eye and a zest for adventure and life. I thought, this is a guy who could be a lot of fun. I've always told my daughters: If you don't have fun with the person you're involved with, then forget it. You have to have fun."

After the night they met, Clarice began concocting excuses to cross paths with Victor. Months went by before she finally came up with a subtle way to approach him, one that was old-fashioned and contemporary at the same time. "I wrote him a postcard and said I'd like to see him again," she remembers. "I could not phone him. At my age that was not acceptable. It was already a step into the next generation that I even contacted him. For me, that was major."

When Victor received the postcard, he wasn't sure who Clarice was at first. But slowly, like a photograph coming clear in a darkroom, he remembered her face and how she had bragged to him at the "lonely hearts" group about climbing a 14,000-foot peak in Nepal. He liked that—he had climbed a few peaks nearly as high in Colorado—so he picked up the phone and called her. On their first date, he cooked her dinner, which they ate in his backyard, next to an elaborate flower garden planted by his ex-wife.

Since then, their children say, they have become a couple hardly anyone can keep up with. They jog together before dawn and take off on long journeys several times a year, often in the style of people fifty years younger. They've slept in caves in Turkey, bicycled through fjords in Nova Scotia, beach-hopped in Mexico. They recently stayed in a mountaintop, feminist-run bed-and-breakfast in Alaska.

"They're so active," said Vicki Lindner. "They're always going sailing and hiking while their middle-aged children trail behind."

Not long after they met, Clarice and Victor traveled to Israel together. On that trip, Victor remembers, he fell in love with Clarice—she was so youthful she still talked about what she wanted to be when she grew up. And Victor had never met anyone so adventurous. "We were walking along the shores of the Gulf of Eilat, and there on the

water was a guy with a motorboat advertising parasailing,"
he remembered. "I took one look at it and turned away very
quickly. But Clarice said, 'I've got to try it.' And before I
knew it, they'd rigged her with a parachute and let her out
with a rope and she was up two hundred feet in the air,
looking down and waving at me. I felt I was being chal-
lenged, so I said, 'Let me go up in that thing!' It looks dangerous and hazardous, but it's not at all—it feels like going
up in a fast-moving elevator in the Empire State Building."

When they're not traveling around the world, Victor and
Clarice can often be found planting flowers in his garden or
on her shady front porch, exchanging stories and memories. "We have so much to talk about," Victor said. "If you're
married to someone for thirty or forty years, you've told
them the same stories over and over, but our old stories are
new to each other, so we don't stop talking for fifteen minutes. It's like a fresh tidal wave of reciprocal conversation,
whereas after a long marriage, it's like, Oh, God, are you
going to tell that story again?"

Occasionally, Clarice and Victor do sound their age
when describing their romance. They talk about how they
worry about each other's health; how she always drives because he tends to drift off the road or forget where he's going. They explain that when you fall in love at their age,
you not only have to ask questions like, Do I like this person's sense of humor? or Can I stand their snoring and their
collection of lava lamps? but also: Do I want this person by
my bedside when I'm dying? When you fall in love in your
seventies and eighties, death is not a terrifying, unthink-

able, far-off thing—it's part of the dinner conversation. Whenever I'm interviewing older couples, I'm always amazed by how unfazed they are about death, how they talk about it so casually, joking about how once the other dies, they'll finally be free to watch David Letterman or leave dirty dishes in the sink. It reminds me of interviewing lobstermen who talk about the bottom of the ocean with familiarity—proximity makes people more comfortable with everything from the ocean floor to death.

But when Clarice and Victor describe how they feel about each other, they sound like a madly-in-love couple of any age. There are certain universals about love stories, I've found, no matter what age a couple is. People tell me over and over that love for them was like a ghost in the room, something ephemeral but unmistakable. In some ways, love *is* like seeing a ghost—you don't ask questions. I think love makes people feel like clairvoyants. Also, I have found that people in love cannot stop complimenting each other. My husband and I have a *New Yorker* cartoon on our refrigerator, with the caption "Feeding time in Egoville." We point to the cartoon whenever one of us feels the need for a compliment. When you're in love, it's *always* feeding time in Egoville.

Whenever I asked Victor about Clarice, he would praise her until I interrupted and changed the subject. "Clarice is very refreshing and delightful," he said one day. "She can strike up a conversation with *anybody*. Also, we have so much in common. No matter where we go or what we do, we find ourselves thinking the same things, almost like telepathic communication. You can't sit around asking yourself what kind of love you're going to find later in life, but I will tell you something: I never expected this."

Whenever I meet couples, I'm always wondering, How in love are they? I've decided asking that question is just as hopeless as looking at the earth in Los Angeles and wondering whether there's an earthquake coming. Love, I'm convinced, is not something you can see on the surface. There are lots of couples who hug and kiss in public—they may *look* madly in love, but I've never believed they're any more in love than couples who walk down the street three feet apart just because that's how they are. A rabbi I once met at a wedding told me, "You can walk down the street holding hands without actually holding hands." I thought that was so romantic, the idea that what's between people is actually more invisible than visible.

One thing I've learned from older couples like Clarice and Victor is that while their hearing may be worse than it once was, or their tennis game weaker, the experience of falling in love isn't muffled or muted with age. Both Clarice and Victor say they fell quickly, deeply, even crazily in love with each other. "There's a freedom in loving Vic that increases the intensity," Clarice said. "It's love without responsibilities. When I married for the first time, I was twenty, and in some ways it's more exciting now. We don't have to worry about our careers or how we're going to bring up the children. So, it's kind of a freebie. The only concern we have is we hope we live to one hundred."

Victor, who introduced Clarice to everything from thrift

shops to canoeing, added, "When you're young, you not only have love but you're beset with problems. You have children driving you crazy, all kinds of little frictions. At our age, most of our emotion can be spent on affection for each other, and it's not diluted by the day-to-day problems. That enhances the potential for a very deep bond, deeper than when you first marry. It doesn't happen with everybody, of course, but it happened with us."

Most of the older couples I've met have had a sense of freedom and lightness about them, a tendency to laugh much more easily than younger couples. I've learned that when people get older, they either cough more or laugh more—they either become sickly and scared or they completely lose their inhibitions. The couples I've known definitely laugh rather than cough more. One elderly couple I interviewed, David Edelstein and Gertrude Bernstein, were both in their eighties when they met and fell in love at a dinner party for widows and widowers given by a friend. David and Gertrude said that while they do almost everything a little slower because of their age, they fell as swiftly and madly in love as teenagers.

"Both of us are walking on air as if we were sixteen years old, although it's been a long time since I was sixteen," David told me. "When I fell in love then, it was all-out, and this is similar, only lighter. It's much more pleasant now than when you're young and all fired up and every imaginary slight can throw you into a funk. We look at each other, we smile. When one does something absentminded, the other one says, 'It's okay, all of us do it.'"

Like Victor and Clarice, David and Gertrude are incredibly young at heart though neither of them wishes they were actually young again. They both yelped "Heavens, no!" when asked if they would rather be in their twenties or thirties. "You laugh more at eighty-one," Gertrude said. "For example, I met David's son for the first time when he came to dinner one night. Now, normally I'm a good cook, but I burned the steak. If that had happened at thirty-five, I probably would have burst into tears, but at eighty-one you see the humor in it."

David and Gertrude got married about six months after they met. When David's friends asked him why he didn't wait any longer, he said, "Are you kidding? At my age, I don't even buy green bananas."

Another telltale sign of love is that it changes you on an almost genetic level—you feel THAT different. In David's case, he never expected to move again in his lifetime—except to the cemetery. Now, instead of living in his apartment filled with brown furniture and books, he is living in Gertrude's aqua-colored, sun-filled apartment.

On July 18, 1998, Clarice and Victor were married on the bride's front porch, which is so long, wide, and breezy, it seems as if it should overlook an ocean. Theirs will be "a modern marriage," the bride said. They wrote their own vows; she will not change her name; and because they enjoy their privacy and space so much, they do not even plan to live together. Unlike younger couples who often don't own much beyond an answering machine and a futon, Clarice and Victor each have a house full of memories, fam-

ily photos, heirlooms, clothes their grown children left behind, tattered-yet-beloved armchairs. "It would take me
years to move out of my house, and I don't have that much
time," Clarice said.

So, the couple commutes back and forth between his
house in Randolph, New Jersey, and hers in Basking Ridge.
"I find it amusing that they have separate houses," said Tom
Olinger, a folksinger and one of Clarice's sons. "Their
houses are like their family foundations. Both have forty or
fifty years of history in those houses. They could be together, but they couldn't quite give up their connection to
those houses and their young family life. We all grew up in
this house, and we still have our own rooms when we come
home. We went through our teenage years here, we listened to rock 'n' roll here, we played touch football on the
huge front lawn."

Though Clarice and Victor fell in love nearly nine years
ago, their houses have changed little since then. For one
thing, neither has removed any photographs or other me-
mentos of their former spouses. "I've looked at pictures of
her husband, she's admired pictures of my wife," Victor
said. "We're both comfortable with each other's homes as
they are. There's no need to say, 'Hey, clean house. I don't
want to see your husband's picture staring at me.' I think I
wouldn't keep pictures in the bedroom—that's my only re-
striction."

Like Clarice and Victor, most of the couples I've interviewed do not seem to hate or resent their significant

other's ex-spouses, ex-boyfriends, or ex-girlfriends as much as you might expect. There seems to be much more peace, even friendship, between present lovers and former ones these days. It's as if that particular cold war is over. "I'm in a situation now where the father of my children and my current partner are really friendly," said Barbara Olinger. "There's no jealousy. My current partner said he loves me, he loves where I've been. He wants to honor that person who spent so much time with me."

I once interviewed an older bridegroom, William Smith, who actually invited his ex-wife and several ex-girlfriends to his second wedding. They all came, in peace. "If someone was wonderful in your life for a period of time, but it didn't work out in the long run, that doesn't mean they suddenly become Darth Vader and the symbol of all evil," William told me. "Why cut a relationship off completely just because it wasn't forever?"

At Clarice and Victor's wedding, you could definitely feel the presence of their exes—pictures of Clarice's deceased husband were even displayed throughout the house. It didn't seem morbid or inappropriate. In fact, it seemed natural that the past should be as much a part of their wedding as the cake and champagne. Love is not an eraser.

The bride and bridegroom's children were all at the wedding, and they are remarkably alike. Most are in their forties now; many have dark wavy hair and turquoise eyes; and they wore wrinkled, baggy linen smocks, Birkenstocks, Indian-print shirts, and other clothes reminiscent of the sixties and seventies. A few were divorced and said their parents' story had given them hope for their own love lives.

"It gives me a sense that love can happen at any age," said Barbara. "I'm kind of going through a parallel thing right now. Even though I'm a single mom with two young kids, I fell in love again. I just turned forty-two and I'm feeling better about myself and the world the older I get. Partly, it's because of my mother as a role model. The enjoyment of life does not decrease just because you get older."

Wendy Gray, another daughter of the bride who runs a Waldorf-inspired day care on Martha's Vineyard, said, "It made me realize you're never done. You can be at the beginning of your life at all times. Also, neither of them is at all like their former spouses. Vic is not at all like my father, and my mother is not at all like Mary, Vic's former wife. You can always reinvent your life. It's never-ending."

Every wedding affects the guests differently. Sometimes, you're left with nothing but a hangover. Other times, weddings inspire you to be more adventurous and ambitious, since every bride and bridegroom makes such an enormous, hopeful, uncertain promise—to stay in love forever. Occasionally, weddings remind you that family and full moons and picnics with friends and beautiful dresses and walking barefoot in the sand are at least as important as your career. But sometimes, a wedding simply reminds you that love does in fact exist. It is real, it can make your heart beat faster than aerobics, and it can change your life completely. That, for me, was the message of Clarice and Victor's wedding.

Watching the couple kissing under the trees, Mayor Hugh Fenwick, who officiated at the wedding, said, "I wouldn't speculate on the bride's age, because gentlemen shouldn't do that. But love can happen anytime, anyplace, anywhere. My advice is: Don't get cynical, don't get jaded. Just believe."

Photo Credits

Photograph of Madeline Mingino and Morty Friedman
by Loretta Drew

Photograph of Susan Chang and Randall te Velde
by Leslie Caroline

Photograph of Lois and William Brady
by Jay Te Winburn

Photograph of Ellen Butler and Eddy Bikales
courtesy of the couple

Photograph of Richelle Sasz and William Neumann
by Peg Neumann

Photograph of Alison Higdon and Peter Boice
by David Wheelock

Photo Credits

Photograph of Susan Stevenson and Richard Woodward
by Thea Reis

Photograph of Mel Schneeberger and Chris Robbins
by Jeff Klausmann

Photograph of Holly Lynton and David Poole
by Karen Hill

Photograph of Linda Lopez and Andre Peters
by Michele Desimone

Photograph of Paisley Knudsen and Karl Schade
by Nan Phelps

Photograph of Clarice Olinger and Victor Lindner
courtesy of the couple

Acknowledgments

My biggest thank-you goes out to all the couples I've interviewed over the years. They let me into their homes, offered me food and drink, told me their love stories and sometimes their entire life stories. They are all here in this book, bits and pieces of their tales, observations, and confessions scattered throughout.

Thanks to the editor of *Love Lessons*, Laurie Chittenden, who reminds me of my favorite brides—she's funny and quirky, she would probably never wear a traditional wedding dress, and she has a great love story: She met her sweetheart, a T-shirt designer who drives a van, on a crowded dance floor in New York City. Her enthusiastic, can-you-believe-it? stories about their romance helped set the tone for this book.

Laurie's calm, competent assistant, Nicole Graev, gave

me great advice on everything from chapter titles to the name of my second son, born partway through writing this book.

Thanks to the editor of "Vows," Bob Woletz, and to the column's phalanx of copy editors—Bernie Kirsch, John Hyland, Shelly Belzer, Steve Coates, Charles McEwen, Charles Klaveness, Christopher Phillips, and Alison Mc-Farland. They polish the column every week and have taught me an important lesson about writing—precision is as important as poetry.

Thanks to my agents, Linda Chester and Joanna Pulcini, who gracefully put up with everything from my slow writing pace to my fear of flying, and still gave me more compliments than I deserved.

Nelly Bly and my sister, Anna Evans, both read drafts of this book and offered incredibly smart suggestions and criticisms. They taught me that just cutting out one weak word can change a whole page. Without them, the book would be flabbier and several notes flatter.

Finally, a working writer is usually not a pretty sight. While writing this book, I often sat at my computer for hours and hours in coffee-stained sweats. If I got really engrossed in the work, I'd sleep in my sweats. Thanks to my husband, Tom, for looking the other way. I promise to go shopping for new clothes soon!

About the Author

Lois Smith Brady has written the popular "Vows" column for *The New York Times* since 1992. Each week in "Vows," she features the ceremonies and love stories of everyone from folksingers to fishmongers, investment bankers, ballerinas, and surgeons. She has also written about love for *Mademoiselle*, *Glamour*, *Cosmopolitan*, and *Esquire*. She lives in Bridgehampton, New York, in an old farmhouse she shares with her husband and their two sons.